BUDDY'S GOT THREE MOMS!

BUDDY'S GOT THREE MOMS!

BY

PETER BAGGE

7563 Lake City Way NE
Seattle, WA 98115

Editorial Co-Ordinbation by Kim Thompson
Design and Art Direction by Carrie Whitney
Inking by Jim Blanchard
Coloring by Jeff Johnson and Joanne Bagge
Cover Colors by Joanne Bagge and Rhea Patton
Published by Gary Groth and Kim Thompson

The material in this collection originally appeared in Hate #21-25.

First Fantagraphics Books edition: June, 1999
Printed in Canada

ISBN 1-56097-335-8

CONTENTS

I'VE GOT THREE MOMS 1
DEAR OLD DAD 25
LISA LEAVENWORTH 46
BABS' EX 47
NOTHING THAT TWENTY YEARS ON THE COUCH COULN'T CURE 71
IT HAD TO HAPPEN 96

MEET THE CAST OF HATE:

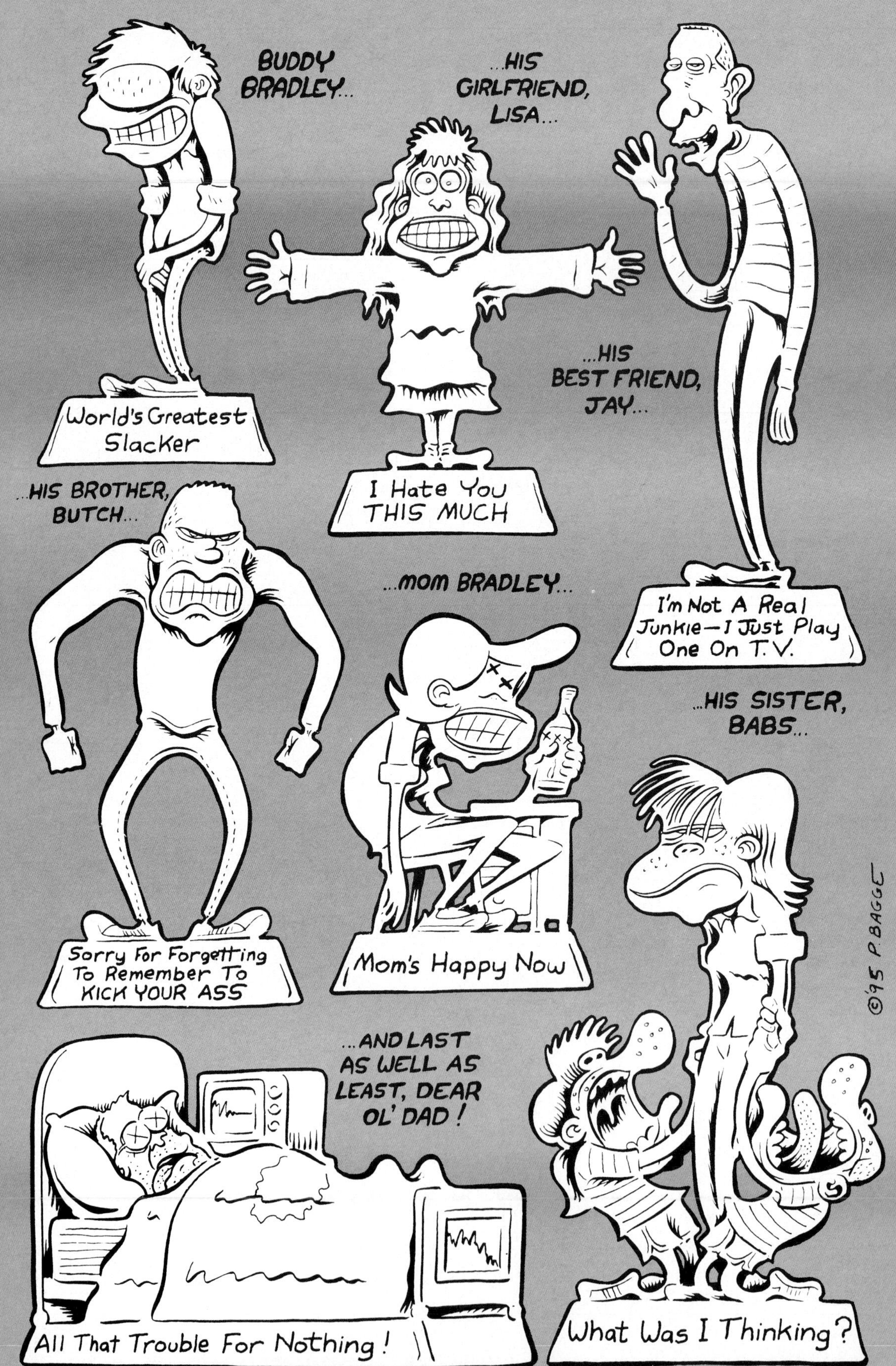

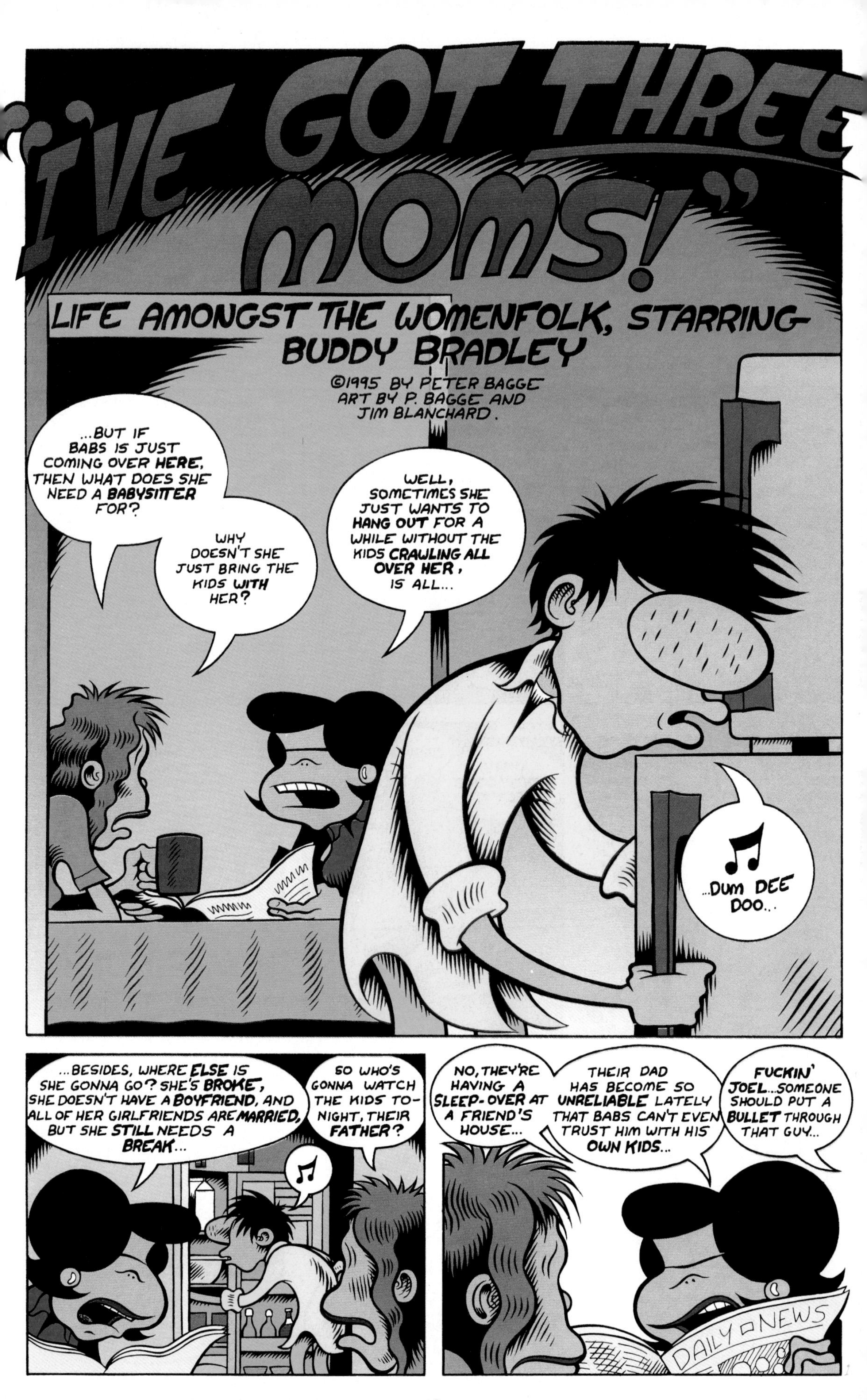

"I'VE GOT THREE MOMS!"

LIFE AMONGST THE WOMENFOLK, STARRING BUDDY BRADLEY

ART BY P. BAGGE AND JIM BLANCHARD.

...BUT IF BABS IS JUST COMING OVER **HERE**, THEN WHAT DOES SHE NEED A **BABYSITTER** FOR?

WHY DOESN'T SHE JUST BRING THE KIDS **WITH** HER?

WELL, SOMETIMES SHE JUST WANTS TO **HANG OUT** FOR A WHILE WITHOUT THE KIDS **CRAWLING ALL OVER HER**, IS ALL...

♫ ...DUM DEE DOO...

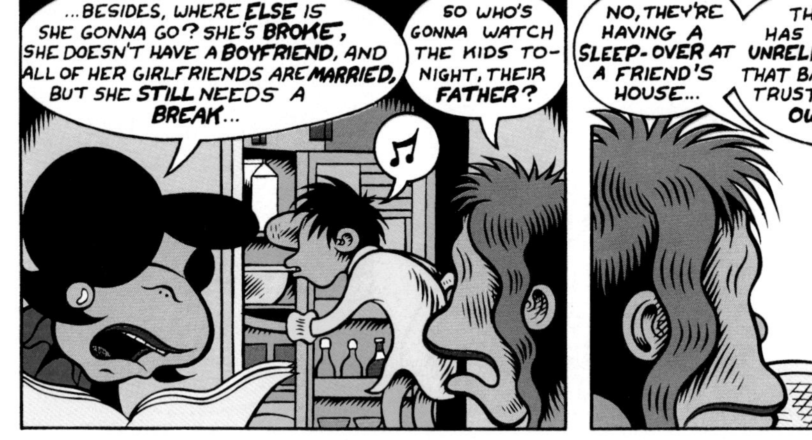

...BESIDES, WHERE ELSE IS SHE GONNA GO? SHE'S BROKE, SHE DOESN'T HAVE A BOYFRIEND, AND ALL OF HER GIRLFRIENDS ARE MARRIED, BUT SHE STILL NEEDS A BREAK...
SO WHO'S GONNA WATCH THE KIDS TO-NIGHT, THEIR FATHER?
NO, THEY'RE HAVING A SLEEP-OVER AT A FRIEND'S HOUSE...
THEIR DAD HAS BECOME SO UNRELIABLE LATELY THAT BABS CAN'T EVEN TRUST HIM WITH HIS OWN KIDS...
FUCKIN' JOEL...SOMEONE SHOULD PUT A BULLET THROUGH THAT GUY...
DAILY NEWS

NOW BUDDY, I DON'T WANT TO HEAR THAT KIND OF TALK—
AND WHY ARE YOU STANDING THERE WITH THE REFRIGERATOR DOOR OPEN? YOU WANT EVERYTHING TO GO BAD?
I'M TRYING TO DECIDE WHAT I WANT FOR LUNCH! ANYTHING WRONG WITH THAT?
MILK

WELL, WHY DIDN'T YOU ASK ONE OF US TO MAKE YOU LUNCH? WE WOULD'VE GLADLY MADE YOU SOMETHING...
YEAH!
HEY, I'M PERFECTLY CAPABLE OF MAKING MY OWN LUNCH!
IT'S NOT EXACTLY BRAIN SURGERY...

SUIT YOURSELF. BUT IT DRIVES ME NUTS THE WAY YOU TAKE FOREVER IN THERE... ...AND YOU ALWAYS LEAVE SUCH A MESS...
I'LL CLEAN UP WHEN I'M DONE, OKAY? DON'T RUSH ME...
SHEESH!
ORTS
DAILY

THERE'S STILL SOME LEFTOVER HOMEMADE CHICKEN SOUP IN THERE, BUDDY...
THERE IS? WHERE?
BREAD

NEVER MIND. JUST HAVE A SEAT AND I'LL MAKE IT FOR YOU...
DON'T DO ME ANY FAVORS! JUST TELL ME WHERE IT IS AND I'LL HEAT IT UP MYSELF!

I'M NOT DOING YOU A FAVOR! I'D JUST RATHER YOU'D STAY OUT OF THE WAY AND NOT MESS UP YOUR MOM'S KITCHEN...
NOW GO SIT DOWN AND I'LL TELL YOU WHEN IT'S READY!
F'R CRYIN' OUT LOUD...

LATER...
OKAY, BUDDY! COME 'N' GET IT!
COMING!
FINALLY!
TIME

MMMM... SMELLS YUMMY...

SLURP! SLOBBER! SLORP!

=AHEM!=
...WELL?
HUH? WELL WHAT?

AREN'T YOU GOING TO SAY THANK YOU?!?
?!?

LATE THAT AFTERNOON...

...WHADAYA MEAN, YA AIN'T GOIN'?
I JUST DON'T FEEL LIKE GOING, THAT'S ALL...
BESIDES, I JUST REMEMBERED THAT I HATE THE YANKEES...
ZZZZZ...

SO WHAT? AT LEAST IT'S SOMETHING TO DO...
...(AND I'M TELLIN' YA, BUDDY, YOU DO NOT WANT TO BE AROUND ONCE BABS STARTS DRINKING... SHE CAN GET PRETTY OBNOXIOUS)...
(I WON'T BE HANGING OUT WITH BABS. I JUST WANT TO SIT HERE AND READ THE PAPER, IS ALL)...

=SIGH=. SUIT YER-SELF...
I'LL BE AT JOEY'S IN CASE YOU CHANGE YOUR MIND...
HAVE FUN...
?

WHAT'S GOING ON? I THOUGHT YOU WERE GOING TO THE GAME WITH BUTCH!
I CHANGED MY MIND.
DAILY NEWS

WHY? I DON'T UNDER-STAND...
HAVE YOU EVER BEEN TO YANKEE STADIUM? IT'S AN INSANE ASYLUM, AND IT'S IN THE WORST NEIGHBORHOOD IN THE WORLD...
SPORTS

OKAY, WHATEVER. I JUST THOUGHT YOU'D ENJOY A "BOY'S NIGHT OUT" FOR A CHANGE, SINCE YOU HARDLY EVER GO ANYWHERE THESE DAYS...
YOU'RE ALWAYS JUST LOLLYGAGGING AROUND THE HOUSE...
OH YEAH, RIGHT, AS IF YOU MIND...
SPORTS

WHAT'S THAT SUPPOSED TO MEAN?
JUST THAT ONCE I COME STAGGERING IN FROM A "BOY'S NIGHT OUT" YOU ALWAYS START IN WITH THE THIRD DEGREE...
"WHERE'D YOU GO?" "WHO WERE YOU WITH?" "WERE THERE ANY WOMEN THERE?" "HOW MANY BEERS DID YOU HAVE?"

I DO NOT!
...DO I?
'FRAID SO, DEAR...
SPORTS

...BUT HEY, I'M NOT GOING ANYWHERE, SO IT'S A MOOT POINT, ISN'T IT?
...NO SENSE WORRYING ABOUT IT...

AN HOUR OR SO LATER...

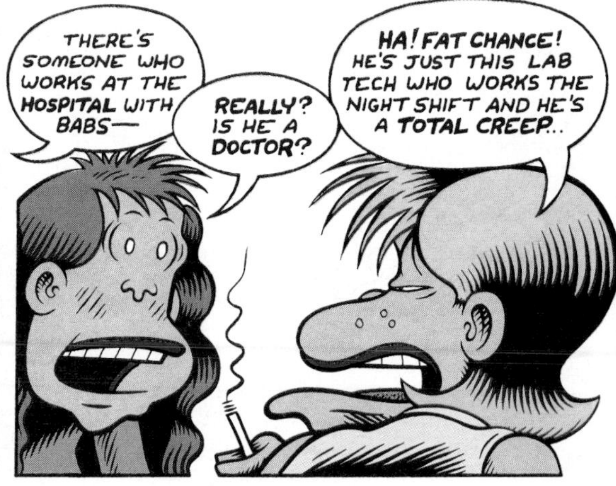

SAY, WHERE'S THAT GODDAMNED PIZZA MAN? HE SHOULDA BEEN HERE BY NOW...
I THINK I JUST HEARD A CAR PULL UP...
I'LL GO CHECK...
YUP, HE'S HERE...
IT'S ABOUT TIME, TOO. I'M STARVING!
WHICH ONE IS IT, LISA? THE ONE WITH THE SHORT BLONDE HAIR, OR THE GREASY FAT KID?
IT'S THE BLONDE, AND HE'S WEARING SHORTS THIS TIME, TOO!
WAHOO! QUICK, OPEN THE DOOR AND LET HIM IN!
HI. YOU ORDERED TWO MEDIUMS WITH PEPPERONI?
SURE DID! COME ON IN!
JUST PLOP 'EM DOWN RIGHT HERE, KIDDO...
THAT'LL BE $22.50, PLEASE...
PAT! PAT!
HERE YA GO, AND KEEP THE CHANGE...
THANKS!
OH, AND BY THE WAY...
...NICE ASS!
WHOA!
PINCH!
BABS! I CAN'T BELIEVE YOU DID THAT!
HA! HA! HA! HA!
(SHEESH, THE POOR KID)...
SLAP!
FLICK!
WHAT DID YOU SAY?
N-NOTHING... LOOK, I, UH, BETTER HURRY AND CATCH UP WITH BUTCH...
HUH? I THOUGHT YOU SAID YOU WEREN'T GO-ING TO THE GAME!
I CHANGED MY MIND AGAIN...
DON'T WAIT UP FOR ME...
SEE YA!
?
SLAM!
HUH! I HOPE HE WASN'T DISAPPOINTED THAT WE ORDERED PIZZA...
FUCK HIM! IF HE WANTS GOURMET CUISINE LET HIM COOK IT HIMSELF...

LATER THAT NIGHT...
KE-RYST! IT'S LATE!
HOPE LISA ISN'T STILL AWAKE...

...DRANK TOO MUCH, TOO...
...I MUST REEK OF BEER...

...LISA PROBABLY GOT DRUNK, TOO, THO' THAT WOULDN'T KEEP HER FROM LECTURING ME ABOUT IT...
NOW TO GET UNDRESSED WITHOUT WAKING HER UP...
ZZZZZ...

SO FAR SO GOOD...NOW TO SLIDE UNDER THE COVERS WITHOUT—
OUCH! MY TOE!
?!? BUDDY? IS THAT YOU?
BANG!

YEAH. SORRY I GOT HOME SO LATE...
NOW GO BACK TO SL—
SO HOW WAS THE GAME? WAS IT FUN?
RUB! RUB!

FEH...
MO VAUGHN HIT TWO HOME RUNS...
IS THAT GOOD?

IT WAS GOOD FOR MO VAUGHN...
...UH, LISA? WHAT ARE YOU DOING?
TAKING YOUR UNDER-WEAR OFF. DO YOU MIND?

N-NO, NOT AT ALL, BUT YOU DON'T HAVE TO—
BUT I WANT TO! NOW BE QUIET WHILE I...

...OHHHHHHH...
SLUMP!
SLORP!

THERE YA GO...
G'DNIGHT, SWEETIE!
G'NIGHT...

?
?
?
ZZZZZ...

NOW **JUST ONE MINUTE!** I DIDN'T— I MEAN I...
IT'S FOR YOUR **OWN GOOD**, DEAR. I JUST DON'T LIKE TO SEE YOU UNDER **SO MUCH STRESS**...
YEAH, **GO SIT DOWN!** YOU'RE MAKING ME A **NERVOUS WRECK!**
I THINK YOU SHOULD **LISTEN** TO HER, MR. BRADLEY...

—BUDDY! BUTCH! GET OVER HERE, QUICK! I NEED BACKUP!
?
!

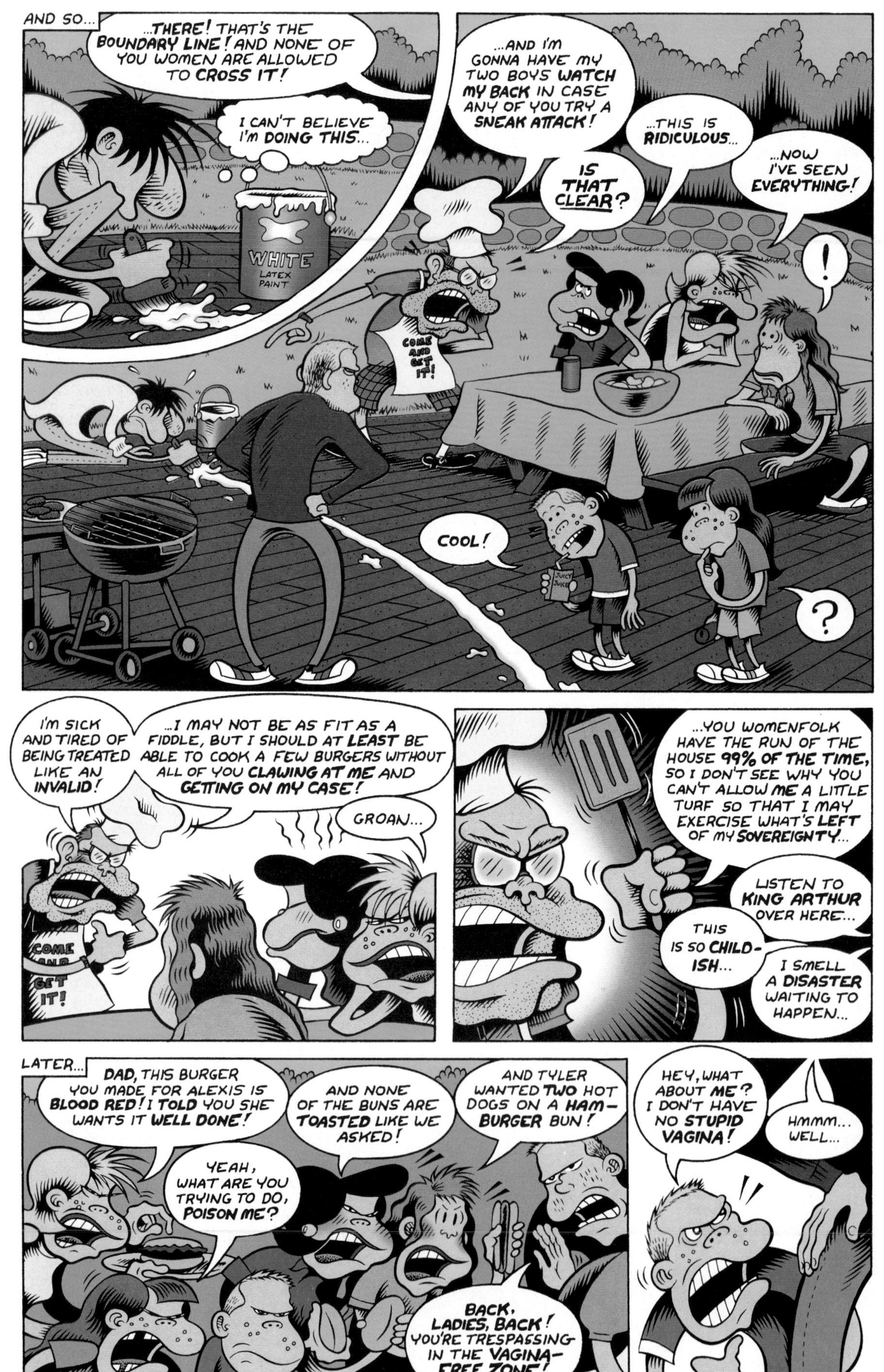
AND SO...
...THERE! THAT'S THE BOUNDARY LINE! AND NONE OF YOU WOMEN ARE ALLOWED TO CROSS IT!
I CAN'T BELIEVE I'M DOING THIS...
WHITE LATEX PAINT
...AND I'M GONNA HAVE MY TWO BOYS WATCH MY BACK IN CASE ANY OF YOU TRY A SNEAK ATTACK!
IS THAT CLEAR?
...THIS IS RIDICULOUS...
...NOW I'VE SEEN EVERYTHING!
!
COME AND GET IT!
COOL!
JUICY JUICE
?
I'M SICK AND TIRED OF BEING TREATED LIKE AN INVALID!
...I MAY NOT BE AS FIT AS A FIDDLE, BUT I SHOULD AT LEAST BE ABLE TO COOK A FEW BURGERS WITHOUT ALL OF YOU CLAWING AT ME AND GETTING ON MY CASE!
GROAN...
...YOU WOMENFOLK HAVE THE RUN OF THE HOUSE 99% OF THE TIME, SO I DON'T SEE WHY YOU CAN'T ALLOW ME A LITTLE TURF SO THAT I MAY EXERCISE WHAT'S LEFT OF MY SOVEREIGNTY...
LISTEN TO KING ARTHUR OVER HERE...
THIS IS SO CHILD-ISH...
I SMELL A DISASTER WAITING TO HAPPEN...
LATER...
DAD, THIS BURGER YOU MADE FOR ALEXIS IS BLOOD RED! I TOLD YOU SHE WANTS IT WELL DONE!
AND NONE OF THE BUNS ARE TOASTED LIKE WE ASKED!
AND TYLER WANTED TWO HOT DOGS ON A HAM-BURGER BUN!
YEAH, WHAT ARE YOU TRYING TO DO, POISON ME?
BACK, LADIES, BACK! YOU'RE TRESPASSING IN THE VAGINA-FREE ZONE!
HEY, WHAT ABOUT ME? I DON'T HAVE NO STUPID VAGINA!
HMMM... WELL...

...OKAY, TYLER, YOU CAN STEP OVER THE LINE, BUT NO ONE ELSE...
HEY! NO FAIR!
OH BOY!

...HOW COME TYLER CAN CROSS THE LINE BUT I CAN'T?
'CUZ YOU'RE JUST A DUMB GIRL, THAT'S WHY!
TYLER, YOU COME BACK HERE THIS INSTANT! YOU'LL GET HURT HOVERING AROUND THAT GRILL!

DON'T LISTEN TO 'EM, TYLER! YOU'RE BETTER OFF WITH US THAN WITH THOSE NAGS...
RAZZ!
RAZZ!

DAD, LOOK OUT! WE'VE BEEN INFILTRATED!
WHAT? WHO? WHERE?

—WHAT DO YOU THINK YOU'RE DOING?!?
I'M JUST TOASTING A FEW BUNS...

GET OUT OF HERE! YOU KNOW THE RULES!
IF THERE'S ANY BUNS TO BE TOASTED THEN I'LL BE THE ONE TO DO IT!
NOW GO ON, GIT!
WELL, I NEVER!

HOW DID THAT HAPPEN? HOW DID SHE GET THROUGH WITHOUT NOTICE?
DON'T LOOK AT ME! SHE SLIPPED THROUGH ON BUDDY'S SIDE!

BUDDY! WHERE WERE YOU?
I WENT IN TO TAKE A LEAK. WHY?

WELL, IT JUST SO HAPPENS THAT WHILE YOU WERE A.W.O.L. OUR SECURITY HAD BEEN BREACHED! ARE YOU AWARE OF THAT FACT?!
NO, BUT... SO WHAT?

"SO WHAT"? ARE YOU THAT UNAWARE OF THE GRAVITY OF THIS SITUATION?
YEAH! HOW ARE WE SUPPOSED TO DO OUR JOBS WHEN YOU'RE AB-ANDONING YOUR POST?

YOU REALLY LET US DOWN, BUDDY...
GOOD GRIEF...

DAYS LATER...
WHAT'S THIS? IS DAD STILL REFUSING TO EAT WITH THE REST OF US?
I'M AFRAID SO...

HE'S STILL FUMING OVER THE "BARBEQUE INCIDENT" LAST WEEKEND...
MAYBE WE SHOULD JUST TELL HIM WE'RE SORRY. I MEAN, IF THAT'S ALL IT'LL TAKE TO GET HIM TO SIT WITH US...

ABSOLUTELY NOT! HE CAN POUT ALL HE WANTS, BUT THERE'S NO WAY I'M GONNA LET HIM SCORE POINTS BY ACTING LIKE A BABY...
I'LL GET IT...
RING! RING!

I DUNNO, MA. IF YOU ASK ME DAD'S GOT A RIGHT TO BE PISSED OFF. HE MAY BE IN BAD SHAPE, BUT HE ISN'T TOTALLY USELESS...
...HE PROBABLY FEELS LIKE HE'S LIVING IN A PLASTIC BUBBLE...
DON'T BE RIDICULOUS! I'M JUST TRYING TO DO WHAT'S BEST...
OH BUDDY, IT'S BABS ON THE PHONE...

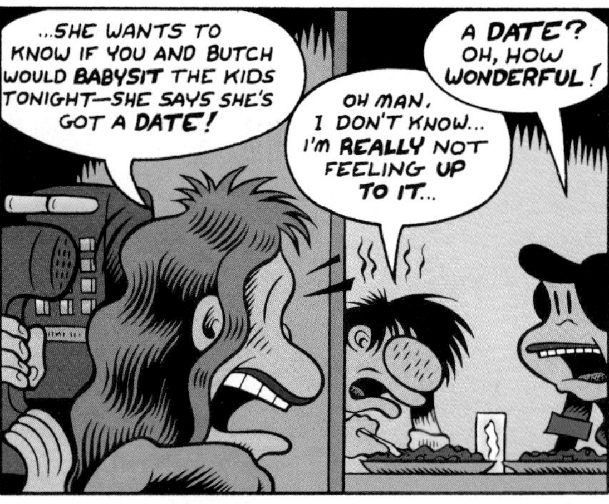
...SHE WANTS TO KNOW IF YOU AND BUTCH WOULD BABYSIT THE KIDS TONIGHT—SHE SAYS SHE'S GOT A DATE!
A DATE? OH, HOW WONDERFUL!
OH MAN, I DON'T KNOW... I'M REALLY NOT FEELING UP TO IT...

OH BUDDY, DON'T BE SUCH A SPOIL SPORT! THIS IS A BIG NIGHT FOR YOUR SISTER!
PLUS THE KIDS LOVE IT WHEN THEIR UNCLES SIT FOR THEM...

YEAH, BUT THOSE LI'L BUGGERS CAN REALLY WEAR ME OUT... I MEAN, YOU HAVE NO IDEA...

OH, I DON'T, HUH? I RAISED YOU, DIDN'T I?
ARRGH...
...BABS SAYS THAT BUTCH IS ALREADY THERE WITH A COPY OF "DIE HARD III", AND THEY'RE GONNA ORDER SOME FRIED RICE AND WON-TON SOUP FROM YOUR FAVORITE CHINESE RESTAURANT...

..HMMM... WONTON SOUP, EH?
HE'LL BE THERE!

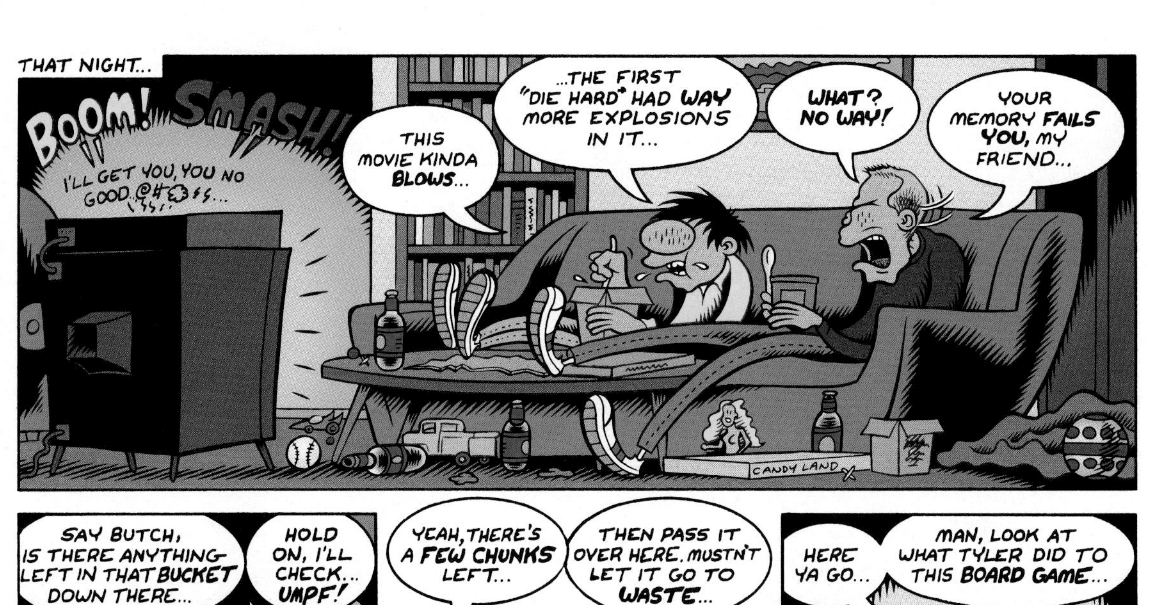
THAT NIGHT...
BOOM! SMASH!!
I'LL GET YOU, YOU NO GOOD..@#✱$$...
THIS MOVIE KINDA BLOWS...
...THE FIRST "DIE HARD" HAD WAY MORE EXPLOSIONS IN IT...
WHAT? NO WAY!
YOUR MEMORY FAILS YOU, MY FRIEND...
CANDY LAND

SAY BUTCH, IS THERE ANYTHING LEFT IN THAT BUCKET DOWN THERE...
HOLD ON, I'LL CHECK... UMPF!
CHOP SUEY LOUIE'S

YEAH, THERE'S A FEW CHUNKS LEFT...
THEN PASS IT OVER HERE. MUSTN'T LET IT GO TO WASTE...

HERE YA GO...
MAN, LOOK AT WHAT TYLER DID TO THIS BOARD GAME...
MADELINE

...SOMEONE NEEDS TO TEACH THAT KID NOT TO BE SUCH A SORE LOSER!
NEVER MIND THE GAME—LOOK AT THIS ROOM! HE COMPLETELY TRASHED THE PLACE!

HMM...DON'T YOU THINK WE OUGHT TO START CLEANING UP?
...THIS IS THE MOST RELAXED I'VE BEEN IN MONTHS...
AAH, FUCK THAT. WAIT 'TIL THE MOVIE'S OVER...

NO SHIT. IT'S NICE TO LISTEN TO THE T.V. WITHOUT DAD SNORING THE WHOLE TIME...
OR HAVIN' MOM AND LISA BUZZIN' ABOUT, INTERRUPTING YOU EVERY FIVE SECONDS...
LET'S GO! RAT-A-TAT-TAT!

...PLUS IT SEEMS LIKE BABS IS OVER EVERY OTHER DAY, AND SHE'S ALWAYS GETTING IN MY FACE ABOUT ONE THING OR ANOTHER...
IT'S LIKE THERE'S NO ESCAPE...
I USED TO HIDE IN THE REC ROOM DOWNSTAIRS UNTIL YOU AND LISA TURNED IT INTO YOUR BEDROOM...
NOW THERE'S NO PLACE TO HIDE...

WHAT WE NEED IS A HANG-OUT OF OUR OWN —A "SANCTUM SANCTORUM," WITH NO WOMEN ALLOWED!
...THE ONLY QUESTION IS WHERE...
WELL, I HAVEN'T GOT A CLUE, AND I DON'T WANT TO FIGURE IT OUT RIGHT NOW...
I'D RATHER NOT THINK FOR A WHILE...
OH, UNCLE BUDDY?...

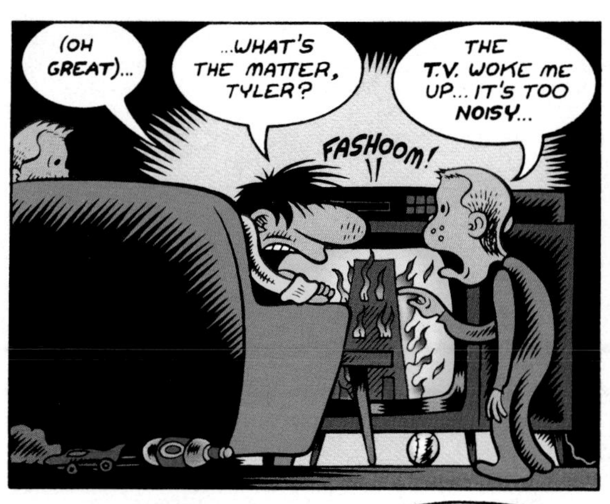
(OH GREAT)...
...WHAT'S THE MATTER, TYLER?
THE T.V. WOKE ME UP... IT'S TOO NOISY...
FASHOOM!

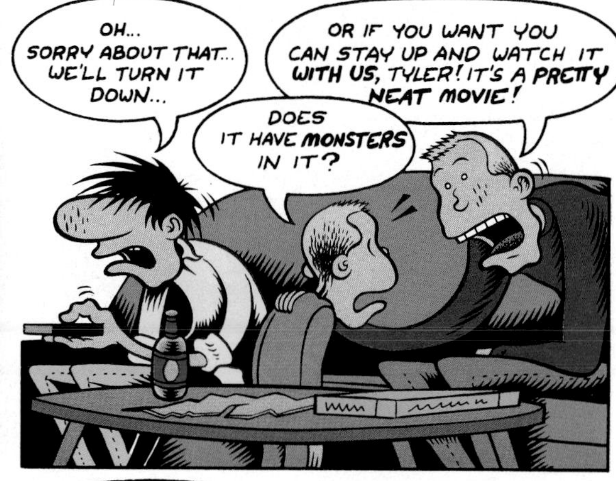
OH... SORRY ABOUT THAT... WE'LL TURN IT DOWN...
OR IF YOU WANT YOU CAN STAY UP AND WATCH IT WITH US, TYLER! IT'S A PRETTY NEAT MOVIE!
DOES IT HAVE MONSTERS IN IT?

NO, NO MONSTERS. JUST A LOT OF MAYHEM...
DOES IT HAVE BAD GUYS IN IT?

...ER, WELL, THERE'S A FEW, BUT THEY'RE NOT TOO SCARY LOOKING, SO DON'T WORRY...
JUST SIT BACK AND GET INTO IT, TYLER! I KNOW YOU'LL LIKE IT, 'CUZ IT'S A REAL GUY MOVIE!
PAT! PAT!

...IS MY MOMMY HOME YET?
NO, BUT SHE'LL BE HOME SOON. NOW KEEP QUIET AND WATCH TH—

I WANT MY MOMMY! WHAAAAAH!
OH, BROTHER...

WHEN'S MY MOMMY COMING HOME? WHERE IS SHE? WHAAAH...
JEEZ, TYLER, WILL YOU CHILL OUT?
YEAH, YOUR MA WILL BE HOME ANY MINUTE!

CLICK! CLACK!
...HELLO? ANYONE AWAKE?
THERE, YA SEE? SHE'S HOME ALREADY!
(THANK GOD FOR THAT)...
LEAP!

TYLER! WHAT ARE YOU DOING UP SO LATE?
UNCLE BUDDY AND UNCLE BUTCH WOKE ME UP BY BEING NOISY!

OH, THEY DID, DID THEY?
(UH-OH, HERE IT COMES)...
(GET READY FOR THE RIOT ACT)...

...AND WHAT THE HELL HAPPENED TO THIS ROOM?!?

NEXT DAY, NEXT DOOR...
SURE, MAN, YOU GUYS CAN COME OVER AND HANG OUT ANY TIME YOU WANT...
...I CAN'T BLAME YOU FOR WANTING TO GET AWAY FROM THE BITCHES...

...IN FACT, FEEL FREE TO BRING YOUR OLD MAN OVER AS WELL. THAT'D BE COOL WITH ME, TOO...
YEAH, WELL, I DON'T KNOW IF ALL THIS POT SMOKING WOULD BE COOL WITH HIM...
...THE JETS ARE ON THE DOLPHINS' 49-YARD LINE...
SSSSSUCK
ROLL, ROLL...

SPEAKIN' O' WHICH, HOW YA DOIN' WITH THAT PIPE, BUTCH? NEED A REFILL?
NAH, IT'S STILL BURNING...BUT HOW DO YOU ADJUST THE COLOR ON THIS BIG SCREEN T.V.? THE GRASS IS TURNIN' BLUE...

THE CONTROLS ARE ALL HIDDEN IN THIS LITTLE COMPARTMENT...
HERE, I'LL SHOW YOU...
?

—OH SHIT! LOOK WHAT YOU JUST DID!!
?!? HUH? WHAT?

YOU SPILLED THE BOWL AND BURNED A HOLE IN THE COFFEE TABLE! HOLY CHRIST, MAN, MY MOTHER'S GONNA FLIP!
WELL, JEEZ, I'M SORRY, MAN! IT WAS JUST AN ACCIDENT...

BUT GOSH, IT DOESN'T LOOK SO BAD TO ME...
SHIT, MAN, YOU DON'T KNOW MY MOTHER...
SHE CARES MORE ABOUT HER FURNITURE THAN SHE DOES ABOUT LIFE ITSELF...

...QUICK, GET ME SOME PINESOL AND WOODGLUE! YA GOTTA HELP ME OUT HERE, MAN!
...OH FUCK, MY MOTHER'S GONNA KILL ME...
...SO MUCH FOR THIS "SANCTUM SANCTORUM"...

FINALLY, THE FOLLOWING WEEKEND...

WELL, IT'S BECOME REAL OBVIOUS TO ME THAT YOU INGRATES HAVE NO APPRECIATION FOR WHAT YOUR MOTHER DOES AROUND HERE!
...YOU DON'T EVEN HAVE A CLUE!
IS THAT SO!?
STOP YAKKIN', BUDDY, AND GET IN THE TRUCK!

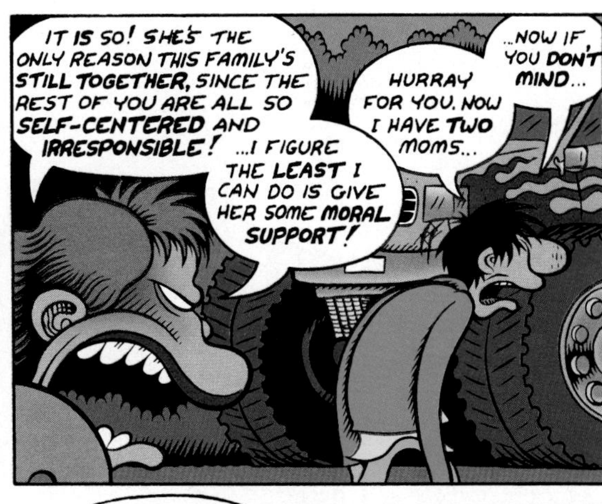
IT IS SO! SHE'S THE ONLY REASON THIS FAMILY'S STILL TOGETHER, SINCE THE REST OF YOU ARE ALL SO SELF-CENTERED AND IRRESPONSIBLE!
...I FIGURE THE LEAST I CAN DO IS GIVE HER SOME MORAL SUPPORT!
HURRAY FOR YOU. NOW I HAVE TWO MOMS...
...NOW IF YOU DON'T MIND...

—BUDDY, DON'T YOU DARE GET INTO THAT TRUCK!
WHAT TH—

JESUS CHRIST, LISA! WHAT'S GOTTEN INTO YOU?!
...SINCE WHEN ARE WE NOT ALLOWED TO LEAVE THE HOUSE!?
I'M SORRY, BUDDY, BUT IT'S NOT YOU —IT'S YOUR FATHER! HE'S A SICK MAN!
...AND I DON'T THINK IT'S A GOOD IDEA FOR YOU TO BE DRAGGING HIM AROUND...

WELL, THAT'S TOO BAD, 'CUZ HE'S MY FATHER, AND I'LL DRAG HIM AROUND ALL I WANT...
WHAT'S IT TO YOU, ANYWAY?
GRRRR...

...IF YOU CARED ABOUT HIM AS MUCH AS I DID YOU'D LET HIM OUT OF THAT TRUCK RIGHT NOW!
FUCK YOU! I'LL DO NO SUCH THING!
BRUM! BRUM!
WHAT'S GOING ON OUT HERE?!
UH-OH...

BUDDY, HOW DARE YOU TALK TO LISA THAT WAY!
BUDDY, IF YOU DRIVE OFF WITH YOUR OLD MAN I SWEAR I'LL NEVER SPEAK TO YOU AGAIN!
(IGNORE THEM, BUDDY! LET'S JUST GET OUT OF HERE, QUICK!)

VRROOOM!
YOU'RE IN BIG TROUBLE, BUDDY BRADLEY!
ADIOS, LADIES!
STOMP! STOMP!
I'VE GOT A BAD FEELING ABOUT THIS...

WHEW! THAT WAS EVEN TOUGHER THAN I THOUGHT IT WOULD BE...
WHAT A COUPLE OF BALL-BUSTERS! JEEZIZ!

...BUT AT LEAST WE GOT AWAY IN ONE PIECE—RIGHT, POP?
...POP?

ZZZZZ...
?!?

JUST A FEW BLOCKS AWAY...

WAKE UP, POP! WE MADE IT TO THE NEAREST WATERING HOLE...
ZZZZZZZK! HUH? "BUSTERS"? I'VE NEVER BEEN HERE BEFORE...
NEITHER HAVE I, BUT WHO CARES? A BAR'S A BAR...
GO KNICKS GO NETS!
Busters SPORTS BAR AND GRILL
LADIES NIGHT TUESDAYS 7-12
PITCHERS $5.00 7-9 pm MON-FRI
FORD
BIGUN

...BUDDY, I CAN'T BELIEVE WE'RE LETTING HIM GET AWAY WITH THAT! I SAY WE GO BACK THERE AND KICK HIS ASS!
RIGHT, HIM AND EVERYONE ELSE IN THAT REDNECK JOINT...
I'M JUST GLAD WE DIDN'T SPEND ANY OF OUR HARD-EARNED MONEY IN THAT PLACE...
I STILL DON'T UNDERSTAND...WHY ARE WE—
Wilting Fern
FORD
TOYOTA

WHAT MADE HIM THINK WE WERE FAGGOTS TO BEGIN WITH? WHAT WAS THAT ALL ABOUT?
YA GOT ME...
FAGGOTS? WHO'S A FAGGOT? WHERE?

OH, WAIT A MINUTE...
...HEY BUDDY, GET A LOAD OF THIS...
HUH? GET A LOAD OF WHAT?
?

THIS! DAD'S SWEATER! IT'S PINK!
NO WONDER THEY THOUGHT WE WERE QUEER! WE WERE LUCKY WE GOT OUT OF THERE ALIVE!
NOW JUST A MINUTE—
GRAB!

YEAH, WHAT IS THE DEAL WITH THAT SWEATER ANYWAY, POPS? DID YOU PUT ON ONE OF MOM'S BY MISTAKE?
OF COURSE NOT! THIS IS MY GOLFING SWEATER! I'VE HAD IT FOR YEARS!

YEAH, WELL, YOU'D BETTER TAKE IT OFF RIGHT NOW, 'CUZ THERE'S NO WAY I'M GONNA BE SEEN WITH YOU—
I WILL NOT TAKE IT OFF!

IT'S PERFECTLY ACCEPTABLE THESE DAYS FOR A MAN MY AGE TO WEAR A SWEATER LIKE THIS...
YEAH, EVERYWHERE EXCEPT "BUSTER'S," APPARENTLY...

=SIGH=...OH WELL... GUESS WE'LL HAVE TO GO TO SOME GAY BAR NOW...
HEY, WHAT ABOUT THAT PLACE RIGHT ACROSS THE STREET?

THAT YUPPIE JOINT? IT LOOKS EXPENSIVE...
MAYBE SO, BUT AT LEAST THEY'RE PROBABLY WILLING TO SERVE A BUNCH OF FAGS LIKE US...
The Wilting Fern

LATER, INSIDE "THE WILTING FERN"...

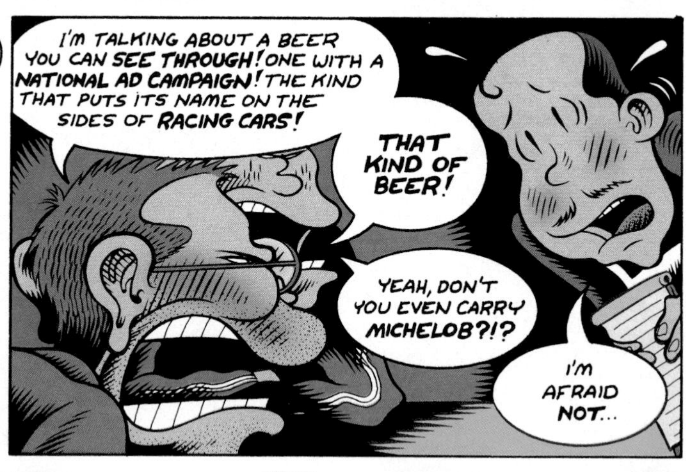

HOURS LATER...
...CAN YOU BELIEVE THAT IRISH PUB WE JUST WENT TO? WE WERE THE ONLY WHITE PEOPLE IN THERE!
AND THE MUSIC IS DEAFENING IN EVERY PLACE WE'VE BEEN TO!
AND WE HAVEN'T STAYED LONG ENOUGH IN ANY ONE PLACE TO EVEN ORDER A BEER!
CLEANERS
FORD
STOP
...BUDDA BUDDA BUDDA...

SCREECH!
—HEY! WHY ARE WE STOPPING?
YEAH, THERE'S NOTHING HERE!

I'M GONNA CALL JAY FROM THIS PAY PHONE AND ASK FOR HIS ADVICE...
JAY?! WHAT DOES HE KNOW?
FORD
MOTHER'S WORRY
LEAP!

OH, YOU'D BE SURPRISED. JAY'S PRETTY KNOW-LEDGEABLE ABOUT THINGS LIKE THIS...
FINE. JUST MAKE IT CLEAR THAT WE'RE LOOK-ING FOR A BAR, NOT AN OPIUM DEN...

...HELLO, JAY? IT'S ME, BUDDY...
YOU'LL NEVER GUESS WHAT I'M UP TO AT THE MOMENT...

...ACTUALLY, IT'S A LONG STORY. BUT I JUST WANTED TO KNOW IF YOU COULD RECOMMEND A GOOD BAR THAT I COULD TAKE MY DAD TO...
OH GREAT...
HEY DAD, WAKE UP!
ZZZzz...

...NO, NOT THAT KIND OF PLACE. JUST A SIMPLE, QUIET PLACE WITH CHEAP BEER...
YEAH, SOMEPLACE OUT OF THE WAY WOULD BE NICE...
PHONE
PHONE

...SO WHERE IS THIS PLACE? TURN RIGHT OFF ROUTE 18...UH-HUH...BEAR LEFT AT SECOND STOP LIGHT... GOTCHA...
ANY LUCK?

...NO, IT'S JUST ME, MY OLD MAN AND MY BROTHER...
SURE, YOU CAN JOIN US... THAT'LL BE FINE WITH ME...
HURRY UP, DAD'S FALLING ASLEEP...
...WHAT DID YOU SAY WAS THE NAME OF THIS PLACE AGAIN?

...IT'S CALLED THE WHAT?!?
?

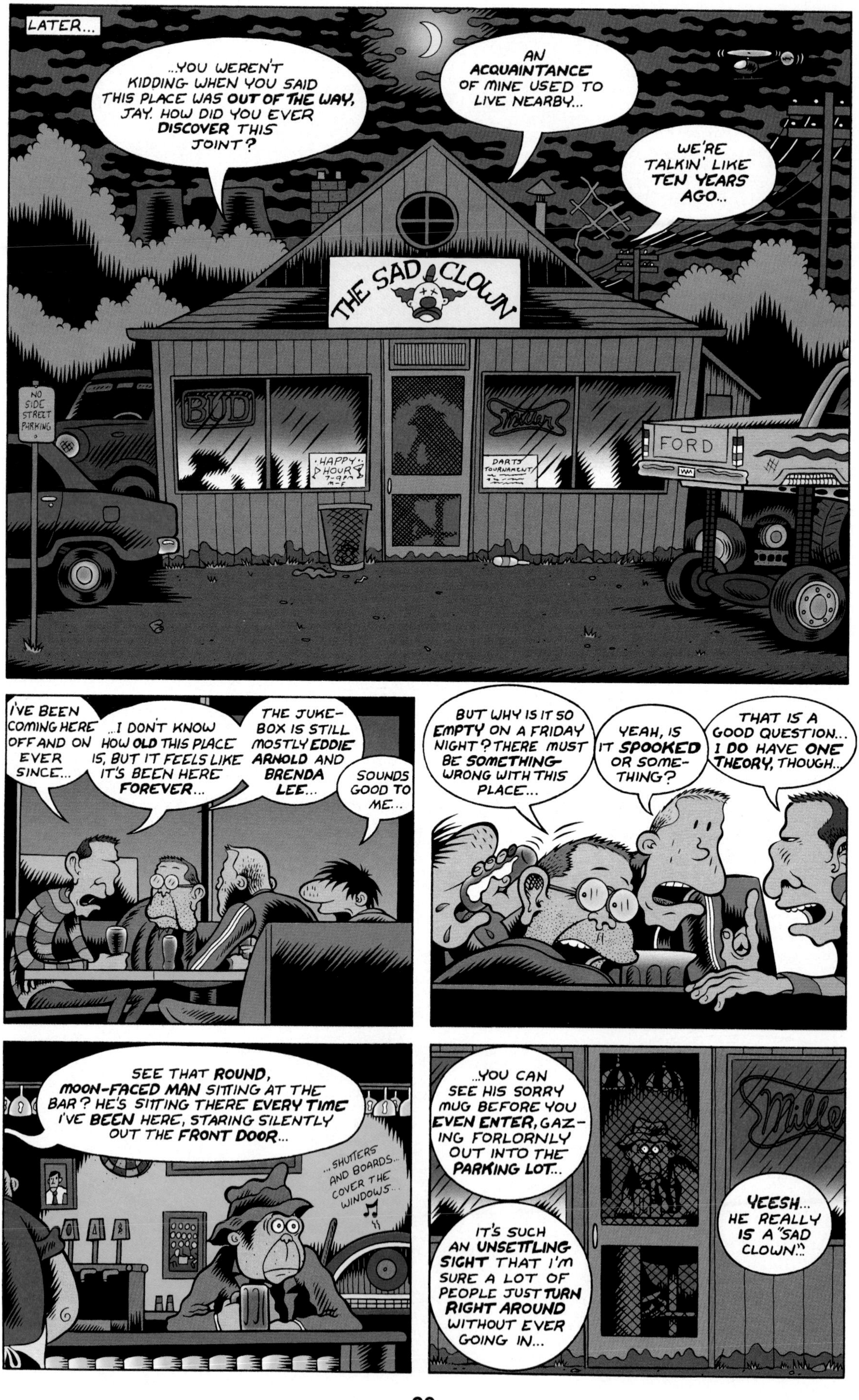

LATER...
...YOU WEREN'T KIDDING WHEN YOU SAID THIS PLACE WAS **OUT OF THE WAY,** JAY. HOW DID YOU EVER **DISCOVER** THIS JOINT?
AN **ACQUAINTANCE** OF MINE USED TO LIVE NEARBY...
WE'RE TALKIN' LIKE **TEN YEARS** AGO...
THE SAD CLOWN
NO SIDE STREET PARKING
BUD
HAPPY HOUR 7-9pm M-F
DARTS TOURNAMENT
FORD

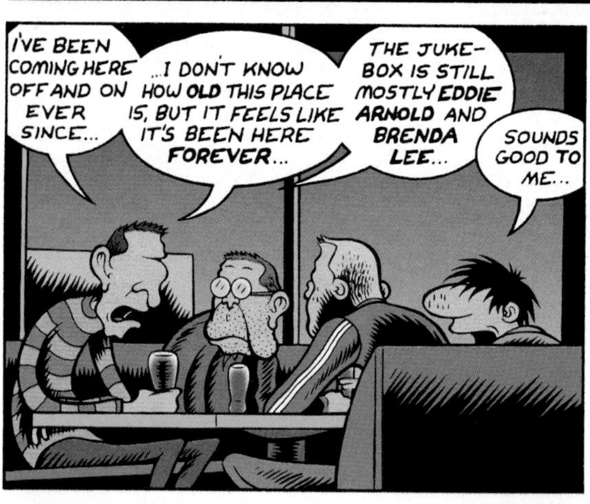
I'VE BEEN COMING HERE OFF AND ON EVER SINCE...
...I DON'T KNOW HOW **OLD** THIS PLACE IS, BUT IT FEELS LIKE IT'S BEEN HERE **FOREVER**...
THE JUKE-BOX IS STILL MOSTLY **EDDIE ARNOLD** AND **BRENDA LEE**...
SOUNDS GOOD TO ME...

BUT WHY IS IT SO **EMPTY** ON A FRIDAY NIGHT? THERE MUST BE **SOMETHING** WRONG WITH THIS PLACE...
YEAH, IS IT **SPOOKED** OR SOME-THING?
THAT IS A GOOD QUESTION... **I DO** HAVE **ONE THEORY,** THOUGH...

SEE THAT **ROUND, MOON-FACED MAN** SITTING AT THE BAR? HE'S SITTING THERE **EVERY TIME** I'VE **BEEN** HERE, STARING SILENTLY OUT THE **FRONT DOOR**...
...SHUTTERS AND BOARDS... COVER THE WINDOWS...

...YOU CAN SEE HIS SORRY MUG BEFORE YOU **EVEN ENTER,** GAZ-ING FORLORNLY OUT INTO THE **PARKING LOT**...
IT'S SUCH AN **UNSETTLING SIGHT** THAT I'M SURE A LOT OF PEOPLE JUST **TURN RIGHT AROUND** WITHOUT EVER GOING IN...
YEESH... HE REALLY **IS** A "SAD CLOWN."

SOUNDS LIKE HE'S BAD FOR BUSINESS... I'M SURPRISED THEY DON'T THROW THE BUM OUT...
YEAH, BUT WHO KNOWS? MAYBE HE OWNS THE PLACE...
LET'S GO TALK TO HIM! MAYBE HE'LL BUY US A ROUND!
NAH...I'D JUST AS SOON KEEP IT A MYSTERY...

...(THOUGH TO BE HONEST, I THINK THE GUY IS RETARDED)...
HAH! JUST LIKE CRAZY GUGGENHEIM!
WHO?

WELL, I DON'T CARE WHAT HIS STORY IS. I JUST HAPPEN TO LIKE EVERYTHING ABOUT THIS PLACE, INCLUDING THE FACT THAT THERE'S NO WOMEN HERE...
HEAR! HEAR! NO BROADS!

...AND AS FAR AS I'M CONCERNED THIS IS JUST THE KIND OF PLACE WE WERE LOOKING FOR—A HOME AWAY FROM HOME...
A "VAGINA-FREE ZONE"! HAW-HAW!
TAP TAP

...SO, WHADAYA SAY, POPS?
HUH? WHAT DO I SAY TO WHAT?

THIS PLACE! DO YOU LIKE IT OR WHAT? SHOULD WE CLAIM IT AS OUR NEW HANG-OUT?
JEEZIZ, I DUNNO...IT DOESN'T HAVE A T.V., AND I HAVEN'T CHECKED OUT THE BATH-ROOM YET...
IT'S CLEAN, AND THE TOILETS ALL WORK. TRUST ME.

=SIGH= ALL RIGHT, WHAT THE HELL...
ALL RIGHT, DAD!
I PROPOSE A TOAST...

...TO OUR NEW SANCTUM SANCTORUM!
CLINK!
HEAR! HEAR!

GLUG! GLUG! GLUG! GLUG!

BLARGH!

DAD! ARE YOU OKAY?
...I TH-THINK YOU'D BETTER GET ME TO A DOCTOR...
SHOOT...HE GOT CHUNKS IN THE PITCHER...

HOURS LATER...

WHAT ON EARTH WERE YOU BOYS THINKING? THAT'S WHAT I'D LIKE TO KNOW...

YEAH, DIDN'T YOU KNOW THAT HE'S NOT SUPPOSED TO MIX ALCOHOL WITH HIS HEART MEDICINE?

NO, WE DIDN'T KNOW!

HOW WERE WE SUPPOSED TO KNOW IF NOBODY TOLD US?

HOSPITAL

PARKING

ENTRANCE

EMERGE

...I CAN'T BELIEVE THE TWO OF YOU! WHEN MOM TOLD ME WHAT HAPPENED I NEARLY DIED!
OH, GREAT. HERE WE GO...
THANKS A LOT, MA...
ZZZZZ...
I WANNA GO HOME...

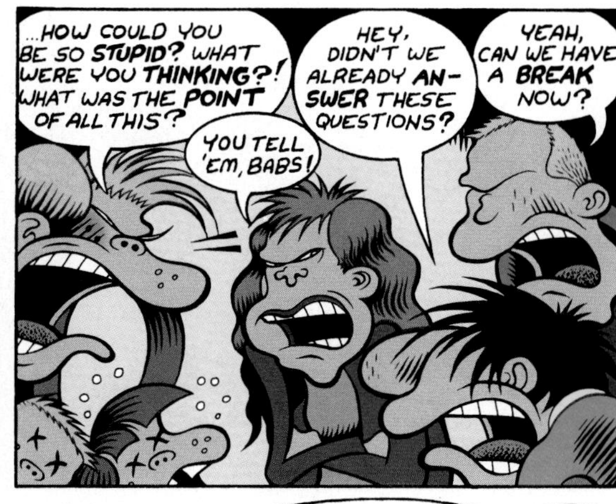
...HOW COULD YOU BE SO STUPID? WHAT WERE YOU THINKING?! WHAT WAS THE POINT OF ALL THIS?
HEY, DIDN'T WE ALREADY ANSWER THESE QUESTIONS?
YEAH, CAN WE HAVE A BREAK NOW?
YOU TELL 'EM, BABS!

HOW'S HE DOIN', MA? CAN WE GO SEE HIM?
HE'S FINE, BUT HE'S ASLEEP RIGHT NOW, SO I—
OH, GET A LOAD O' THIS! LOOK WHO'S SO CONCERNED FOR DEAR OLD DAD ALL OF THE SUDDEN!

WHAT'S THAT SUPPOSED TO MEAN?
CAN THE ACT, BABS! YOU HATE DAD, AND EVERYBODY KNOWS IT!
YOU HATE ALL MEN, THAT'S YOUR PROBLEM!

WHAT?!? WHY, LISTEN TO YOU, YOU...YOU WOMAN-HATER! YOU MACHO, SEXIST, ALCOHOLIC NAVY REJECT!
WHY YOU—

HALP! =ACK! ACK!=
...I OUGHTA SHUT YOU UP FOR GOOD...
BUTCH! CONTROL YOURSELF!
PEOPLE, PLEASE!

...THIS IS A HOSPITAL, FOR GOODNESS SAKES! PLEASE SHOW SOME CONSIDERATION!
I'M SORRY, NURSE...
WE'LL BE QUIET...
=ACK!= =COUGH!= =HACK!=

= SIGH = WELL, AT LEAST WE KNOW YOUR FATHER WILL BE ALL RIGHT...
...LET'S ALL GO BEFORE WE CAUSE HIM ANY FURTHER EMBARRASSMENT...
OKAY, MA...
BABS IS THE ONE WHO'S ALWAYS CREATING A SCENE...
LOOK WHO'S TALKIN', YA BIG APE!
DIBS ON THE FRONT SEAT!
NO WAY!

=WHEW!= GOOD RIDDANCE!
NOW I CAN FINALLY GET SOME PEACE...
I LOVE HOSPITALS...

WEEKS LATER...
HERE'S YOUR DINNER, DEAR... I HOPE IT'S NOT TOO HOT...
WOULD YOU LIKE ME TO RE-ADJUST YOUR CHAIR, "DAD"?
NO THANKS, LISA. I'M FINE...
...THE GIANTS ARE LOOKING PRETTY GOOD IN THE FIRST HALF...
JEEZ, LOOK AT THIS! IT'S PATHETIC!
HE DOES LOOK PRETTY HELPLESS, DOESN'T HE?

WE SHOULD KIDNAP HIM AND BRING HIM BACK TO THE "SAD CLOWN," ONLY THIS TIME WE'LL MAKE SURE HE DOESN'T TAKE HIS MEDICINE...
OH, SURE, AND THIS TIME INSTEAD OF JUST THROWING UP HE'LL HAVE A MASSIVE HEART ATTACK...
OH, WHAT A HIT!

SO WHAT ARE YOU SAYING, THAT WE GIVE UP ON HIM?
WELL, YEAH! IT'S OBVIOUS THAT HE'D RATHER SIT HERE AND BE PAMPERED THAN STEP OUT INTO THE BIG BAD WORLD AGAIN...

WELL THEN, HOW ABOUT JUST US GOIN' OUT?
WE NEVER WENT BACK TO THAT PLACE LIKE WE SAID WE WOULD...
I KNOW, BUT...

BUT WHAT?!? C'MON, LET'S BUG OUT OF THIS MATERNITY WARD RIGHT NOW! WHADAYA SAY?
I, UH...
OH, BUDDY...

...SORRY TO INTERRUPT, BUT I HEATED UP YOUR FAVORITE T.V. DINNER FOR YA: LEMON CHICKEN WITH CORN, SPANISH RICE AND VANILLA PUDDING...
OH BOY! YELLOW FOOD!

...AND YOUR DAD'S GONNA WATCH "NAKED GUN 33⅓" ONCE THE GAME'S OVER, SO WHY DON'T YOU SIT RIGHT HERE AND MAKE YOURSELF COMFY?
MMMM... SOUNDS LIKE A PLAN...
?!?

I'LL GET YOU SOME LEMONADE— OR WOULD YOU RATHER HAVE A BEER?
LISA, WILL YOU TURN UP THE VOLUME ON THE T.V.? MY REMOTE MUST NEED NEW BATTERIES OR SOMETHING...
(PSST! HEY, BUDDY!)

HMM? OH YEAH, WHAT WERE WE TALKING ABOUT AGAIN? I FORGOT...
NOTHING. SKIP IT...

...THE POWER OF THE PUSSY STRIKES AGAIN!

END.

BUDDY BRADLEY AND HIS GALPAL LISA

in

DEAR OLD DAD

DRAWN BY P. BAGGE AND JIM BLANCHARD

ISN'T THERE SOMEPLACE BESIDES THE **MALL** WHERE WE CAN GET OUR CHRISTMAS SHOPPING DONE?

WHY? WHAT'S WRONG WITH THE **MALL**?

TONIGHT ON "HARD COPY"...

HOLD ON A MINUTE, YOU GUYS...
=TSK!= NOW WHAT?

...ARE YOU OKAY, "DAD"? IS ANYTHING WRONG WITH YOUR ARM?
HMM? OH, IT'S NOTHING...

...IT'S JUST A LITTLE NUMB, IS ALL...
=GASP!= THAT ISN'T NOTHING! THAT COULD BE SERIOUS!
OH BROTHER...

WHADAYA MEAN, "SERIOUS"?
WELL, ISN'T THAT ONE OF THE WARNING SIGNS? FOR, LIKE, A HEART ATTACK?
ALRIGHT, LET'S NOT ALARM OURSELVES...
=GASP!=

...NOW TELL ME, BRAD, HOW EXACTLY DOES YOUR ARM FEEL...
IT'S FEELING ALL NUMB AND TINGLY, LIKE WHEN IT'S FALLING ASLEEP...
=GASP!= MAYBE HE'S HAVING A STROKE!

LISA, WILL YOU STOP! FOR GOODNESS SAKES...
SORRY...

WELL, WHADAYA THINK, BRAD? SHOULD WE BE CONCERNED?
DO YOU WANT ME TO CALL A DOCTOR?
YEAH, HURRY UP AND DECIDE IF YOU'RE DYING OR NOT, 'CUZ WE GOTTA GET TO THE MALL BEFORE IT CLOSES...
BUDDY! YOU'RE TERRIBLE!

NAH, I'M OKAY... IT'S PROBABLY JUST FROM LACK OF USE THAT IT FEELS THIS WAY...
YOU GUYS GO ON AHEAD... DON'T WORRY ABOUT ME...
ARE YOU SURE? YOU'RE NOT JUST SAYING THIS, ARE YOU?
WHO CARES IF HE IS? LET'S JUST GO...

...Y'KNOW, BRAD, I SURE WISH YOU'D GO SEE THAT PHYSICAL THERAPIST YOUR DOCTOR RECOMMENDED...
"PHYSICAL THERAPIST"— BAH! WHAT GOOD'LL THAT DO ME?

WELL, FOR ONE THING HE COULD SHOW YOU HOW TO KEEP IN SHAPE WITHOUT PUTTING TOO MUCH STRAIN ON YOUR HEART...
...THAT WAY YOU MIGHT AVOID BECOMING A VEGETABLE...
HEY, WE COULD ALWAYS PICK UP A WORK-OUT VIDEO FOR HIM WHILE WE'RE OUT...
HOW ABOUT "BUNS OF STEEL"? I HEAR THAT'S A GOOD ONE...

?!?
WHAT? WHA'D I SAY?

:SIGH: FORGET IT...
JUST GET IN THE CAR, MISTER WISE-ACRE...
YOU TOO, LISA...
I'M NOT GOING...

-HUH?
WHAT DID YOU SAY?
I SAID I'M NOT GOING...

...I THINK SOMEONE SHOULD STAY HERE TO KEEP AN EYE ON DAD...
BESIDES, THERE'S NO REASON FOR ME TO GO...
PAMELA SUE MARTIN'S PLASTIC SURGEON TELLS ALL!!

BUT THERE'S NO REASON FOR YOU TO STAY, EITHER!
C'MON, LISA! DAD'LL BE FINE BY HIMSELF...
NO! I'M STAYING AND THAT'S THAT!
WILL YOU PEOPLE KEEP IT DOWN? I CAN'T HEAR THE T.V...

LET HER STAY, BUDDY... I'LL BE IN THE CAR...
DON'T KEEP YOUR MOTHER WAITING, BUDDY...

...(DON'T DO THIS TO ME, LISA! I DON'T WANT TO GO SHOPPING WITH MY MOTHER BY MYSELF)...
WELL, WE HAVE TO GET OUR CHRISTMAS SHOPPING DONE SOONER OR LATER...

I'M JUST TRYING TO BE PRACTICAL, BUDDY...
AND DON'T WORRY ABOUT ME. I DON'T MIND STAYING...
WELL, OKAY... WHATEVER...

...IT'S BECAUSE YOU WANT TO STAY THAT I'M WORRIED...
ZZZZ...

NEXT DAY...
ADAMS PEANUT BUTTER

DUM DEE DOO...
SOUNDS LIKE THE **GAME** IS ON...
THE OILERS LINE UP ON THEIR OWN 37...

?!?
WHAT TH—

LISA! WHAT ARE YOU **DOING?**
(SHH! BE QUIET!)
...(I'M GIVING HIM SOME **PHYSICAL THERAPY**)...
ZZZZ...

"PHYSICAL THERAPY"? I THOUGHT HE **COULDN'T BE BOTHERED** WITH THAT STUFF...
THAT'S WHY I'M TRYING TO DO IT WHILE HE'S **ASLEEP**...
IT'S IMPORTANT TO KEEP HIS MUSCLES IN **WORKING ORDER**...

IT **IS**, HUH? AND HOW DID **YOU** BECOME AN **EXPERT** ON THE SUBJECT?
I ASKED YOUR **SISTER**, SINCE SHE'S A **NURSE**. SHE SAID A PATIENT COULD SUFFER FROM **"ATROPHY"** IF THEY DON'T USE THEIR **LIMBS**...
CHOMP!
ZZZZZ

I SEE... SO NOW HE'S YOUR **"PATIENT"**... NOW I'VE SEEN **EVERYTHING**...
SO WHAT'S IT TO **YOU** IF I'M TRYING TO HELP HIM? IT'S NO SKIN OFF **YOUR** NOSE...

THAT'S RIGHT, IT **ISN'T**...
...THOUGH WATCHING YOU HANDLE MY OLD MAN'S **FLESH** IS KINDA **GROSSING ME OUT**...
OH, **YOU**...

...I SUPPOSE YOU'D BE PERFECTLY WILLING TO **CHANGE HIS BED PAN** AS WELL, SHOULD IT EVER COME TO **THAT**...
WELL, **SURE**, WHY NOT? THAT'D BE **NO BIG DEAL**...
ZZZZ...

—HEY, WHERE ARE YOU **GOING**? I THOUGHT YOU WERE GONNA WATCH THE GAME...
I'M GONNA HAFTA EAT THIS IN **ANOTHER ROOM**...
=GAG!=

ONE WEEK LATER...
...THE NAUGHTY LADY OF SHADY LANE... ♫
MUSTAR

♪ DUM DEE DOO...
...SOUNDS LIKE THE GAME IS ON...
...OOOH, THE FANS DON'T LIKE **THAT** CALL...

WHO'S PLAYING?
BEARS VS PACKERS...
NO SCORE SO FAR...

=SNIFF= =SNIFF=
WHATCHA GOT THERE? **ROAST BEEF?**
CLOSE. **HAM ON RYE.**
CHOMP!

SMELLS GOOD...IS THAT BREAD **FRESH**?
JUST BOUGHT IT THIS MORNING FROM THE **NEIGHBORHOOD DELI**...
CHOMP!

...SAY, UH, YOU WOULDN'T MIND MAKING **ONE** OF THOSE FOR **ME**, WOULD YA?
I KNOW IT'S NOT ALLOWED ON MY NEW, **STRICT DIET**, BUT—
HEY, EAT WHATEVER YOU **WANT**. I PROMISE NOT TO **SQUEAL**...
...THIS IS JOHN MADDEN SAYING ACE IS THE PLACE...

...ONLY YOU'LL HAVE TO MAKE IT **YOURSELF**, SINCE I'M NOT YOUR **SLAVE**...
WHAT?
OH, C'MON, DON'T GIVE ME A **HARD TIME**! I'M JUST ASKING FOR THIS **ONE FAVOR**...

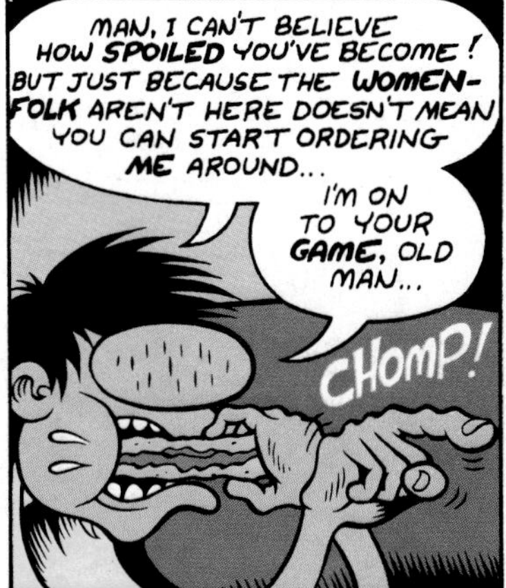
MAN, I CAN'T BELIEVE HOW **SPOILED** YOU'VE BECOME! BUT JUST BECAUSE THE **WOMEN-FOLK** AREN'T HERE DOESN'T MEAN YOU CAN START ORDERING **ME** AROUND...
I'M ON TO YOUR **GAME**, OLD MAN...
CHOMP!

...MAYBE IF YOU GOT **UP OFF OF YOUR BUTT** A LITTLE MORE OFTEN YOU WOULDN'T BE IN SUCH **DIRE NEED** OF "PHYSICAL THERAPY" —DIDJA EVER THINK OF **THAT**? =SLOBBER= =CHEW=
ARRRGH...

...UMMPF!
?!?
GRUNT...

WHOA, GET A LOAD OF THIS!
IT'S SIMPLY AMAZING WHAT A MAN'LL DO WHEN A LOAF OF FRESH RYE BREAD IS AT STAKE...
...HEH, HEH...
OOF!

...HEH, HEH, HEH...
WOBBLE... TODDLE...

FLUMP!
?!?

OMIGOD!
DAD! ARE YOU ALRIGHT?

SHIT! I CAN'T EVEN TELL IF HE'S ALIVE OR NOT!
MAYBE IF I FLIP HIM OVER...

...UMMPF! JEEZUZ...I HOPE I NEVER TURN INTO A TUB OF LARD LIKE THIS...
HE WOULD HAVE TO KEEL OVER WHEN I'M THE ONLY ONE HOME...
LURCH...

HMMMM... I THINK I HEAR A HEARTBEAT, THOUGH IT'S HARD TO TELL UNDER ALL THIS BLUBBER...
MAYBE IF I POUND ON HIS CHEST...

POUND!
-OW! HEY! STOP THAT!

DAD! WHAT HAPPENED TO YOU?
...I DUNNO... I GUESS I PASSED OUT FOR A FEW SECONDS...
...BUT MAYBE YOU SHOULD CALL 911, JUST TO PLAY IT SAFE...

SURE, POPS, WHATEVER YOU SAY...
OH, AND BUDDY...

YES, DAD? WHAT IS IT?
...WHO ARE YOU CALLING A TUB OF LARD...

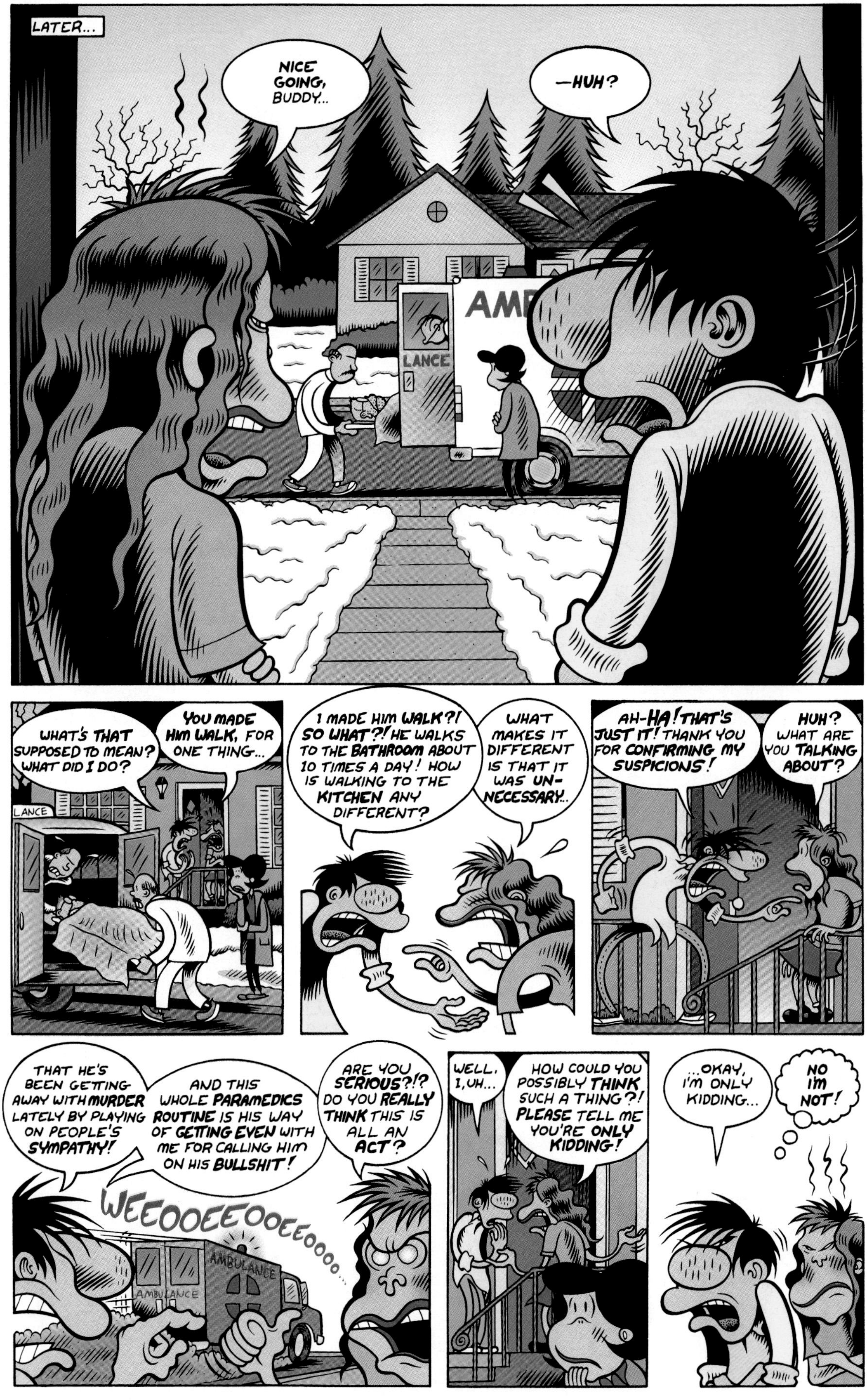

LATER...

NICE GOING, BUDDY...

—HUH?

AMB

LANCE

A FEW DAYS LATER...
...SO HOW'S THE OLD MAN DOING? IS HE STILL IN THE HOSPITAL?
HE SHOULD BE COMING HOME TODAY, SO I GUESS HE'S OKAY...
...AS LONG AS NO ONE FORCES HIM TO MAKE HIS OWN SANDWICHES, THAT IS...
COMICS COMICS
Casper
TOY COLLECTOR SWAP MEET
WHAM! UK
RANDY RANDY
NOV. 11 GLASS BUFFER
Action Suits
EDGAR WINTER GROUP VS KISS
SGT. ROCK
FUN
BOOM BOOM

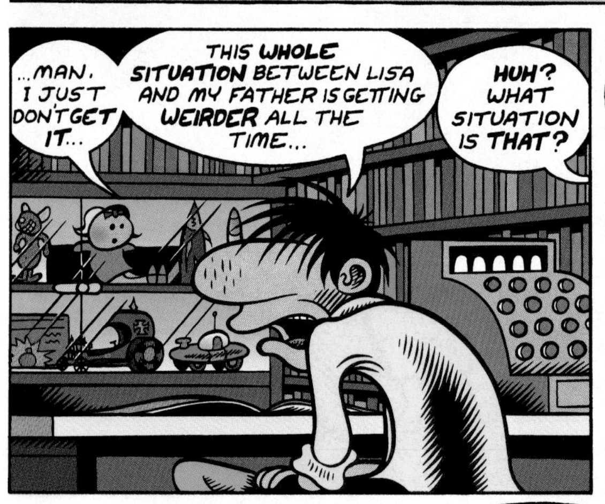
...MAN. I JUST DON'T GET IT...
THIS WHOLE SITUATION BETWEEN LISA AND MY FATHER IS GETTING WEIRDER ALL THE TIME...
HUH? WHAT SITUATION IS THAT?

OH, JUST THE WAY SHE DOTES ON HIM, AND WAITS ON HIM HAND AND FOOT...
SHE EVEN GIVES HIM MASSAGES —I'M TELLIN' YA, IT'S PERVERSE!
YEESH... IS HE PAYING HER TO DO THIS?
CHARMING, IMPRACTICAL VINTAGE REGISTER

NO! IN FACT SHE'S TOTALLY INTO IT!
SHE'D PROBABLY PAY HIM TO LET HER DO IT!
HMMM... CURIOUS BEHAVIOR INDEED...

...ALTHOUGH IT COULD SIMPLY BE THAT SHE'S RATHER FOND OF THE OLD COOT, AND IS JUST TRYING TO MAKE LIFE EASIER FOR HIM...
OH, IT GOES WAY BEYOND THAT! SHE'S OBSESSED!
SHE WON'T EVEN LEAVE THE HOUSE ANYMORE UNLESS MY MOTHER'S HOME—SHE'S CONVINCED SOMETHING BAD'LL HAPPEN IF SHE DOES...
HMMMM...

WELL THEN, LET ME ASK YOU THIS: WHAT DOES LISA DO ON HER DAYS OFF? DOES SHE HAVE ANY FRIENDS? OR HOBBIES?
ERRR... NO, SHE DOESN'T HAVE EITHER, ACTUALLY...

...AND THE TWO OF YOU HARDLY EVER GO OUT ANYMORE, DO YOU...
NO... IN FACT IT'S BEEN AGES...

SO IN OTHER WORDS, THE POOR GIRL DOESN'T HAVE A LIFE...
PERHAPS YOU SHOULD TAKE THAT INTO CONSIDERATION...
=GULP!=

THAT EVENING...

WHAT'S SO FUNNY, LISA?
YEAH, FILL US IN!
AH-HA-HA-HA-HA-HA...
OH, GOD... =GASP=
ZZZZZZZ...

YOUR FATHER STARTED TO MUMBLE SOMETHING UNINTELLIGIBLE WHILE WATCHING "WHEEL OF FORTUNE," SO I LEANED IN CLOSER AND ASKED HIM TO REPEAT HIMSELF, JUST IN CASE IT WAS SOMETHING IMPORTANT...
WHAT'D HE SAY?
YEAH, SO?

SO HE POINTS TO THE T.V. SCREEN AND SAYS: "VANNA WHITE'S TITS ARE MADE OUT OF CARDBOARD", AND THEN FALLS RIGHT TO SLEEP!
HAW! HAW! HAW! HAW!

SLAP!

OH FOR GOODNESS SAKES...

...OH MAN, WHAT A SCREAM...
HAW, HAW, HAW...
UH, LISA...

...I THINK YOU AND I SHOULD HAVE A LITTLE TALK...
?!? A "TALK"? ABOUT WHAT?

"WHEEL OF FORTUNE," FOR ONE THING...
"WHEEL OF FORTUNE"?—HEY, DID YOU KNOW THAT'S YOUR FATHER'S FAVORITE SHOW?

I KNOW, AND I DON'T HAVE A PROBLEM WITH THAT...
WHAT BOTHERS ME IS THAT YOU ALWAYS WATCH IT WITH HIM, NIGHT AFTER GODDAMNED NIGHT...
OH YEAH? SO WHAT'S IT TO YOU? WHAT DO YOU CARE? IT'S NO SKIN OFF Y—

OKAY, I KNOW! THAT'S NOT THE POINT...
THEN WHAT IS YOUR POINT?

WHAT'S MY POINT?
...SHIT, I FORGOT WHAT MY POINT WAS...
?

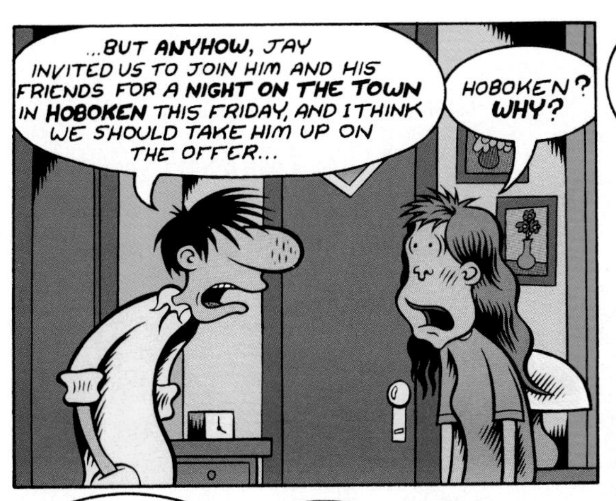
...BUT ANYHOW, JAY INVITED US TO JOIN HIM AND HIS FRIENDS FOR A NIGHT ON THE TOWN IN HOBOKEN THIS FRIDAY, AND I THINK WE SHOULD TAKE HIM UP ON THE OFFER...
HOBOKEN? WHY?

"WHY"?!? BECAUSE IT'S SOMETHING TO DO, THAT'S WHY!
REMEMBER HOW A LONG TIME AGO YOU AND I USED TO GO OUT EVERY ONCE IN A BLUE MOON? REMEMBER THOSE DAYS?
YEAH, SO?

SO, LET'S DO IT AGAIN, OKAY? JUST FOR OLD TIMES' SAKE!
OH, JEEZ, I DUNNO...

NO OFFENSE, BUT I'M REALLY NOT ALL THAT INTERESTED IN HANGING OUT IN SOME TRENDY, OVER-PRICED BAR WITH JAY AND HIS JUNKIE LOSER FRIENDS...
IT JUST SOUNDS LIKE A BIG WASTE OF TIME TO ME... SORRY...
OH...WELL THEN, HOW ABOUT JUST YOU 'N' ME—

PLUS I'D HATE TO LEAVE YOUR FATHER ALONE BY HIMSELF IN THE EVENING...
...I FEEL LIKE HE REALLY DEPENDS ON MY COMPANY THESE DAYS...
ARRRGH! WILL YOU STOP WORRYING ABOUT MY FATHER!
ZZZZzz...

LOOK AT HIM! DOES HE LOOK LIKE HE'S REVELLING IN YOUR PRESENCE AT THE MOMENT? HMMM? DOES HE?!?
OH, HE'S JUST TAKING A LITTLE CAT NAP...
BUT WHAT IF HE WOKE UP AND I WASN'T HERE?
AND WHAT ABOUT HIS CONDITION? WHAT IF—
ZZZzoRK!

ENOUGH! I DON'T WANT TO HEAR IT!
WE'RE GOING OUT WITH JAY THIS FRIDAY NIGHT AND THAT'S FINAL! AM I MAKING MYSELF CLEAR?
YES, SIR...

GOOD! ...I'M SURE YOU WON'T REGRET IT, EITHER...
A NIGHT ON THE TOWN WILL PROBABLY DO YOU A WORLD OF GOOD...
HEARTLESS BASTARD!
ZZZNUCK!

THAT FRIDAY NIGHT...

...YOU GUYS **ARE** GONNA LISTEN TO OUR BAND PLAY LATER, AREN'T YA? I'LL PUT YOU ON THE **LIST**...

UHHH... I **DUNNO**, WE'LL HAVE TO SEE...WHAT KIND OF MUSIC DO YOU **PLAY**?

MAXWELL'S

...POOR GUY... HE'S REALLY NERVOUS. THIS IS THE FIRST TIME OUT FOR HIS NEW ROCK COMBO...
YOU CAN TELL HE WANTS TO BE A ROCK STAR IN THE WORST WAY...
IT'S REALLY KIND OF SAD...
WHO TOLD THAT GUY I WAS IN A ROCK BAND? DID YOU?!
DID I?! OF COURSE NOT!
JESUS CHRIST, LISA, WILL YOU STOP ACTING SO DEFENSIVE?

...HEY, WHO ARE THOSE WEIRDOS HE'S TALKING TO NOW? ARE THOSE HIS BANDMATES?
I DOUBT IT... MAYBE IT'S HIS FAN CLUB...

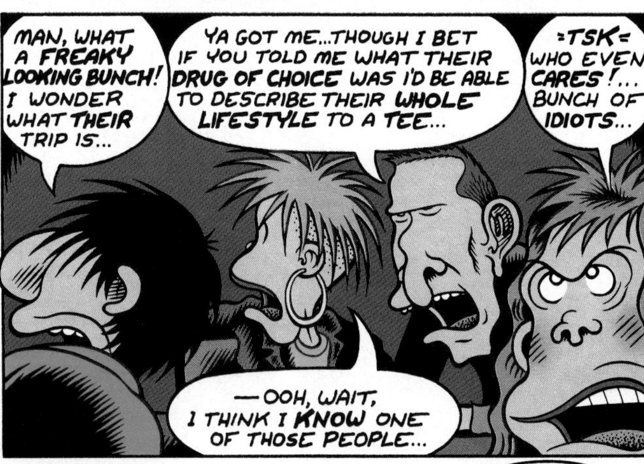
MAN, WHAT A FREAKY LOOKING BUNCH! I WONDER WHAT THEIR TRIP IS...
YA GOT ME...THOUGH I BET IF YOU TOLD ME WHAT THEIR DRUG OF CHOICE WAS I'D BE ABLE TO DESCRIBE THEIR WHOLE LIFESTYLE TO A TEE...
=TSK= WHO EVEN CARES!... BUNCH OF IDIOTS...
—OOH, WAIT, I THINK I KNOW ONE OF THOSE PEOPLE...

REALLY? WHICH ONE?
THE GAL WITH THE NOSE RING. REMEMBER HER, JAY? SHE USED TO DANCE AT THE CLUB I WORK AT YEARS AGO...
...LAST I HEARD SHE WOUND UP DOING PORNO FLICKS...

...AT LEAST IT'S NICE TO SEE SHE SURVIVED THAT RACKET IN ONE PIECE...
SHE WAS A PORN STAR? WHAT'S HER NAME? MAYBE I KNOW HER "WORK"!

=TSK!= LISTEN TO YOU...
BUT HER NAME'S STACY... DON'T ASK ME WHAT HER "STAGE NAME" WAS...
INTRO-DUCE US! I'LL ASK HER MYSELF!

DON'T YOU DARE! YOU CAN COME WITH ME TO SAY HI, BUT ONLY IF YOU PROMISE NOT TO ACT LIKE A PIG...
I PROMISE! LET'S GO!

WHERE DO YOU THINK YOU'RE GOING?

?!? WHO, ME? I WAS JUST—
YOU THINK YOU'RE GONNA LEAVE ME SITTING HERE BY MYSELF WHILE YOU RUN OFF TO SLOBBER OVER THAT TRAMP? FAT CHANCE, BUSTER!
HI, STACE! REMEMBER ME?
OH, HI!!!!!!!

BUT I...
OH, FORGET IT!
SLUMP!

BOY OH BOY, LISA...IF I KNEW YOU WERE GOING TO BE THIS WAY I NEVER WOULDA ASKED YOU TO COME ALONG...
BUT YOU DIDN'T ASK ME—YOU FORCED ME, REMEMBER?

OH YEAH, THAT'S RIGHT. I FORCED YOU... AND NOW YOU'RE PUNISHING ME FOR IT, IS THAT IT?
HEY, I'M NOT ACTING THIS WAY ON PURPOSE! BUT HOW CAN I NOT BE MISERABLE SITTING HERE IN THIS HELL HOLE?

IT'S NOT A "HELL HOLE"! IT'S A BAR, WHERE PEOPLE COME TO DRINK, TALK AND RELAX...
IT'S A BAR FULL OF PHONIES AND POSEURS IS WHAT IT IS!

:SIGH: ALRIGHT, SO IT IS, BUT SO WHAT?
ISN'T THAT HALF THE FUN OF COMING TO A PLACE LIKE THIS? TO SIT AND MAKE FUN OF EVERYBODY? WE USED TO DO IT ALL THE TIME...
THAT WAS THEN, THIS IS NOW. NOW I'VE GOT BETTER THINGS TO DO...

YEAH, LIKE SITTING AT HOME AND WATCHING JEOPARDY WITH A DECREPIT OLD GEEZER, FOR EXAMPLE...
THAT'S RIGHT, FOR EXAMPLE!

SLUMP!

...I DUNNO, LISA, I JUST CAN'T FIGURE YOU OUT... NOT THAT I EVER COULD, BUT...
SO WHY BOTHER TRYING?

"WHY BOTHER", INDEED... I THINK I SHALL GIVE UP TRYING, 'CUZ I'VE PRETTY MUCH HAD IT WITH YOU...
—HUH?

WHADAYA MEAN, YOU'VE "HAD IT"?!
WHAT I MEAN IS YOU'RE A FUCKING NUT, AND I'M SICK OF PUTTING UP WITH YOUR INSANITY!
THAT'S WHAT I MEAN!

...ERRR...I, UH, DIDN'T MEAN TO PUT IT QUITE THAT WAY...

OH, GREAT...

LISA, WAIT! I DIDN'T MEAN TO—
LEAVE ME ALONE! I'VE HAD IT WITH YOU, TOO!

HOLD UP, WILL YA? I SAID I'M SORRY!
LET GO OF ME, YOU—
GRAB!

LEMME JUST ASK YOU ONE THING...
WHAT? HURRY UP AND ASK!
WHAT EXACTLY IS THE DEAL WITH YOU AND MY OLD MAN? I MEAN, YOU ARE SO INTO LOOKING AFTER HIM THAT I—
BECAUSE IT MAKES ME FEEL LIKE A GOOD PERSON, THAT'S WHY!

HUH? BECAUSE Y—
FOR THE FIRST TIME IN MY LIFE I FEEL USEFUL AND NEEDED, AND NOT JUST SOME TAG-ALONG LAUGHING-STOCK WHO'S TAKING UP SPACE!

...OH... I SEE... BUT—
AND I ONLY WISH YOU CARED ABOUT YOUR FATHER AS MUCH AS I DO! THAT'S SOMETHING I'D LIKE TO UNDERSTAND!

HEY, I CARE ABOUT MY OLD MAN, BUT NOT TO THE POINT WHERE I'M HOVERING AROUND HIM ALL DAY, CATERING TO HIS EVERY WHIM!
HMPF!

I'M THE ONE WHO GREW UP WITH THE GUY, REMEMBER? AND I STILL GOT BUMPS ON MY HEAD TO REMIND ME OF WHAT HE USED TO BE LIKE!
THERE'S JUST TOO MUCH HISTORY BETWEEN US FOR ME TO FEEL THE PURE, UNADULTERATED PITY THAT YOU SEEM TO FEEL FOR HIM...

BESIDES, LOOK AT HOW DISCONNECTED YOU ARE FROM YOUR OWN FAMILY!
WHEN WAS THE LAST TIME YOU EVEN TALKED TO YOUR PARENTS? LAST CHRISTMAS?
=GULP!= I, UH... DON'T REMEMBER...

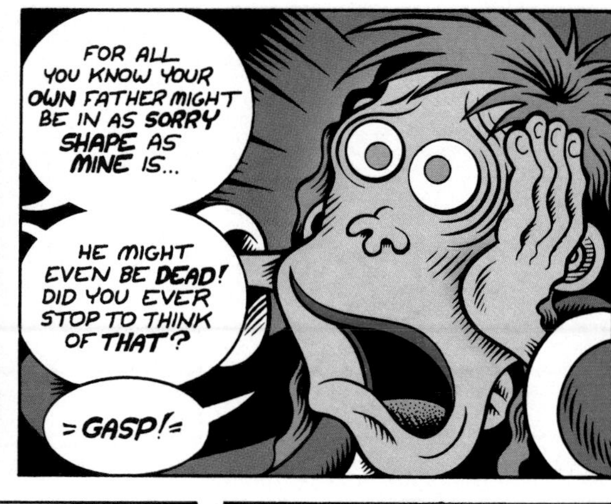
FOR ALL YOU KNOW YOUR OWN FATHER MIGHT BE IN AS SORRY SHAPE AS MINE IS...
HE MIGHT EVEN BE DEAD! DID YOU EVER STOP TO THINK OF THAT?
=GASP!=

OH MY GOD! I REALLY AM A TERRIBLE PERSON! YOU MUST THINK I'M SUCH A PHONEY...
NAH... I UNDERSTAND WHY YOU'D WANT TO DISTANCE YOURSELF FROM YOUR OWN RELATIVES...
BELIEVE ME, I UNDER-STAND...

...SO I'M NOT TRYIN' TO DUMP ON YA—I'M JUST TRYING TO MAKE YOU SEE WHERE I'M COMIN' FROM WITH THIS WHOLE "DAD" THING...
NO, I GET THE PICTURE ALL RIGHT... LOUD AND CLEAR...

...SO I GUESS YOU'RE EAGER TO GO BACK INSIDE TO MEET THE PORN STAR...
WHILE WE GROOVE TO A LOUDER, SLOWER VERSION OF THE CLASH? NOT REALLY...

...BUT JAY'S PROBABLY LOOKING ALL OVER FOR US RIGHT NOW, SO—
THERE YOU ARE! I WAS LOOKING ALL OVER FOR YOU GUYS!

WE, UH, JUST STEPPED OUT FOR SOME FRESH AIR...
...SAY, ISN'T YOUR FRIEND'S BAND GOING ON SOON?
THEY'RE PLAYING RIGHT NOW, AND MAN DO THEY SUCK!
THEY SOUND LIKE KISS!

THAT'S TOO BAD...
YEAH, SO THE EX-PORN STAR INVITED US TO JOIN HER AND HER FRIENDS FOR A GAME OF INDOOR MINIATURE GOLF!
WHADAYA SAY? YA WANNA?

WELL?
SURE, WHAT THE HECK!
GREAT!

...BY THE WAY, BUDDY, I FOUND OUT WHAT THEIR DRUG OF CHOICE IS...
OH YEAH? AND WHAT'S THAT?

PAINT THINNER!
HOW EXCELLENT...

NEXT MORNING...

MY, LOOK AT YOU! YOU SEEM RATHER SPRIGHTLY THIS MORNING!
YES, AND YOU'RE ALL DRESSED UP AND EVERYTHING!
SLOBBER!
MUNCH!

AHH!
YES, AND I'M FEELING RATHER SPRIGHTLY THIS MORNING AS WELL...
WIPE

IN FACT, I'M FEELING AS FIT AS A FIDDLE!
LEAP!
I HAVEN'T FELT THIS GOOD IN AGES!
WELL WHOOP-DEE-DO!
GLAD TO HEAR IT!

AND SINCE I'VE GOT SO MUCH ENERGY TO BURN, I THINK I'LL GO FOR A NICE LONG STROLL...
WHAT?!

G-GEE, POP, ARE YOU SURE THAT'S A GOOD IDEA? I MEAN—
ARE YOU KIDDING? IT'S A GREAT IDEA!
JUST LOOK OUTSIDE—THE SUN IS SHINING, THE BIRDS ARE SINGING...
YA DON'T GET MANY DAYS LIKE THIS THIS TIME OF YEAR, SO WHEN YA DO YA GOTTA TAKE ADVANTAGE OF IT!

PLUS A BLAST OF FRESH AIR WOULD DO ME A WORLD OF GOOD—
DON'T YOU AGREE?
I, UH... SUPPOSE...

WELL, SEEING HOW YOUR MIND IS MADE UP, HOW ABOUT IF I COME ALONG WITH YOU...
YES, WHY NOT LET BUDDY JOIN YOU?
NONSENSE!
ZOOM!

I'M SURE YOU BOTH HAVE BETTER THINGS TO DO THAN TO CHASE AFTER ME!
BESIDES, I'M LOOKING FOWARD TO THIS OPPORTUNITY TO COLLECT MY THOUGHTS...
SEE YOU LATER!
BUT...

SLAM!

OH, WELL...

LATER...

WHERE THE HELL IS HE? HE'S BEEN GONE FOR A WHOLE HALF-HOUR ALREADY!
WHERE'D HE DECIDE TO WALK TO, PENN-SYLVANIA?!?
WILL YOU RELAX? A HALF-HOUR ISN'T ALL THAT LONG...

IN FACT, YOU SHOULD BE THRILLED THAT HE'S FEELING SO CHIPPER...
MAYBE HE'S TURNED A CORNER, AND HIS HEALTH REALLY IS ON THE MEND...
I DON'T KNOW... I JUST DON'T HAVE A GOOD FEELING ABOUT THIS...
TAP! TAP! TAP!

=TSK!= NOW YOU'RE SOUNDING LIKE YOUR MOTHER...
IF SHE WERE HERE I'M SURE SHE'D BE SAYING THE SAME THING I AM...
IF SHE WERE HERE SHE WOULDA NEVER LET HIM LEAVE THE HOUSE, WHICH IS WHAT WE SHOULDA DONE!
SALE

WILL YOU STOP!
...HERE, WHY DON'T YOU SIT HERE AND READ THE PAPER WHILE I PUT S'MORE COFFEE ON...
NO MORE COFFEE FOR ME, THANKS. THAT'S THE LAST THING I NEED AT THE MOMENT...

FINE. I'LL JUST MAKE SOME FOR MY-SELF...
RING! RING!
UT, THERE'S THE PHONE... I'LL GET IT...
WHERE'S THE SPORTS SECTION? ...OH WELL...

...JEEZIZ... HOW CAN ANY-ONE RELAX BY READING THE PAPER?
IT'S CHOCK FULL OF WAR, MURDER AND MAYHEM!
AFRICA STARVES TO DEA
RACK ADDICTS TAKE OVER WHITE HOUSE

BUT LISA'S RIGHT, I AM GETTING CARRIED AWAY WITH MY WORRYING...
I OUGHT TO STOP...
YES, I'LL TELL HIM...
...THANK YOU. BYE.

?!? WHAT'S UP WITH YOU, LISA?
YOU LOOK AS THOUGH YOU'VE JUST SEEN A GHOST...

THAT WAS THE POLICE...
YOUR FATHER WAS HIT BY A TRUCK AND WAS KILLED INSTANTLY...

THREE DAYS LATER...
MOM, I'M BORED!
ME TOO! AND I'M HUNGRY!
FUNERALHOME
HEAVENLY HILLS FUNERAL HOME
NO UNAUTHORIZED PAR
FORD

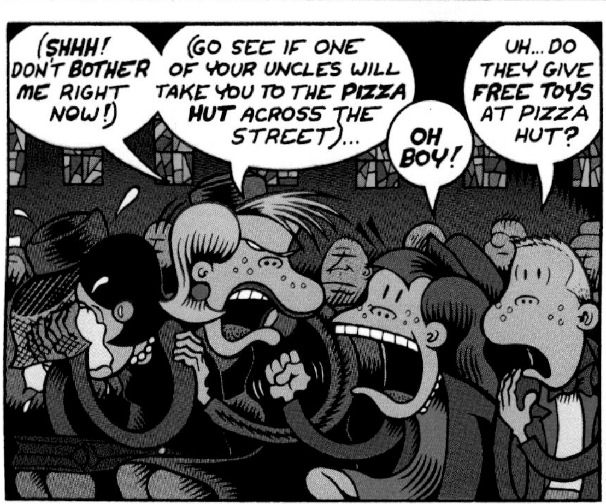

(SHHH! DON'T BOTHER ME RIGHT NOW!)
(GO SEE IF ONE OF YOUR UNCLES WILL TAKE YOU TO THE PIZZA HUT ACROSS THE STREET)...
OH BOY!
UH... DO THEY GIVE FREE TOYS AT PIZZA HUT?

...(I DON'T SEE WHY MY MOM HAD TO INSIST ON A CLOSED CASKET...)
(HIS FACE WASN'T THAT MESSED UP...)
YEAH, WELL...
HEY, UNCLE BUTCH!
R.I.P.

MEANWHILE...
...DEARLY BELOVED... LET US NOT FEEL SORROW FOR THE RECENTLY DEPARTED, FOR HE IS IN A BETTER PLACE...

(...WHAT? WHY DO YOU KEEP LOOKING AT ME LIKE THAT?)
(HUH?... OH, I'M SORRY, I DIDN'T MEAN TO—)

(IS IT BECAUSE YOU'RE AFRAID I'M GONNA CRACK-UP NOW THAT MY "TICKET TO HEAVEN" HAS PASSED AWAY?)
NO, IT'S JUST THAT... ERR... WELL, YEAH, I AM...
HEY, UNCLE BUDDY!

WILL YOU TAKE US TO THE PIZZA PLACE ACROSS THE STREET? PUH-LEEEZE?
MOM SAID YOU HAVE TO!
YEAH, WE ASKED UNCLE BUTCH BUT HE SAID NO, THE BIG STINKER!
=SIGH=... ALL RIGHT, I'LL TAKE YA...

YAY!
C'MON! LET'S GO!
YOU WANNA COME ALONG?
SURE, I'M KINDA HUNGRY MYSELF...

...ANYHOW, BUDDY, DON'T WORRY ABOUT ME... I'LL BE ALL RIGHT...
ARE YOU SURE?

ABSOLUTELY, BECAUSE AT LEAST I KNOW THAT I HELPED TO MAKE HIS FINAL DAYS A LITTLE EASIER...
HMMM...
AND THAT THERE'S AT LEAST ONE PERSON I'LL ALWAYS KNOW I NEVER BAILED-OUT ON...
C'MON, YOU GUYS!
YEAH! YOU'RE WALKIN' WAY TOO SLOW!

...PLUS NOW THAT HE'S GONE HE WON'T BE A SOURCE OF CON-TENTION BETWEEN THE TWO OF US...
OY, NOW YOU'RE MAKING ME FEEL GUILTY...

...BUT WHAT I'M ALSO CONCERNED ABOUT IS WHAT YOU'RE GONNA DO WITH YOUR SPARE TIME, NOW THAT YOU'VE LOST YOUR MAIN HOBBY...
...OH... I DUNNO... I'LL THINK OF SOMETHING...
TYLER! YOU FORGOT TO LOOK BOTH WAYS!
EXIT

BUT I WANT TO WARN YOU OF ONE THING, AND YOU HAVE TO PROMISE NOT TO GET MAD WHEN I TELL YOU...
OH? AND WHAT'S THAT?

...THAT I INTEND TO KEEP WATCHING "WHEEL OF FORTUNE"...
HEY! THEY'RE CLOSED!
OH NO! NOW WE'RE GONNA STARVE TO DEATH!
RATTLE! RATTLE!
END.

LISA LEAVENWORTH, AT YOUR SERVICE!

EXCUSE, ME, MISS...
YES?

ARE YOU FAMILIAR WITH THIS MOVIE? I'M DEBATING WHETHER OR NOT I SHOULD RENT IT...
HMMM...

...OH! OH! THIS MOVIE HAS THAT GUY IN IT! I JUST SAW THIS GREAT OLD MOVIE WITH HIM IN IT!
OH? WHICH MOVIE WAS THAT?

OH SHIT, WHAT WAS IT CALLED...IT ALSO STARRED THAT OTHER GUY—YOU KNOW, THAT DUDE WHO USED TO STAR IN ONE OF THOSE COP SHOWS FROM THE SIXTIES...
WHO? WHICH—

...THERE WAS THIS GREAT SCENE IN IT WHERE HE'S IN THIS WEIRD CASTLE WHERE ALL THESE NAKED LADIES ARE WALKING AROUND WHO ARE, LIKE, HALF DEAD OR SOMETHING...
REALLY?

OH! OH! AND TOWARDS THE END THIS GUY TRIES TO KISS ONE OF THE DEAD BABES AND HIS FUCKIN' HEAD EXPLODES! IT WAS FUCKIN' HILARIOUS! HAW! HAW!
I, UH...
SLAP!

SHIT, MAN, WHAT WAS THE NAME OF THAT FRIGGIN' MOVIE...SHIT, SHIT, SHIT...
UH, LOOK, I, UH...
BONK! BONK! BONK!

AAH, FUCK IT, I CAN'T REMEMBER...

OH, BUT THAT MOVIE'S REALLY GOOD, TOO. YOU SHOULD GET IT!

in

BABS' EX

DRAWN BY P. BAGGE
AND JIM BLANCHARD

...UGHHH... IS IT **MORNING** ALREADY? I FEEL **GROSS**...

...GROANN... I FORGOT HOW MUCH I **HATE** CAMPING....

HEY NOW, DON'T START TRYING TO MAKE ME FEEL GUILTY—
YEOW! THIS SUN IS BLINDING!

...AND LOOK AT THIS MESS WE MADE LAST NIGHT!
OH, WHAT FUN WE'RE GONNA HAVE CLEANING THIS UP!
YUCK... I GUESS THIS WASN'T SUCH A HOT IDEA AFTER ALL, HUH?
CHIPS

YEAH, WELL, NO SENSE IN DWELLING ON IT...
...MIGHT AS WELL GET TO WORK...
OHHHH... I FEEL LIKE SHIT...
KICK!

...WHAT WOULD HAPPEN IF WE JUST LEFT IT LIKE THIS? WOULD WE GET FINED?
I DUNNO. I—
YO! BUDDY BRADLEY!
CHIPS

?!?
WHO SAID THAT?
YO! OVER HERE!

...(OH NO)...
...(WHAT'S THE MATTER? WHO IS THAT?)
WELL, WELL, WELL! FANCY MEETING YOU AROUND THESE PARTS, EH, BUDDY?
ARE WE A SIGHT FOR SORE EYES OR WHAT?

...LISA, THIS IS MY EX-BROTHER-IN-LAW, JOEL...
JOEL, THIS IS LISA...
PLEASED TO MEET YA...
OH, UH, HI...
?!?

...SO YOU'RE BABS' EX-HUSBAND?
IN THE FLESH! THOUGH WE SHOULDN'T TALK TOO MUCH ABOUT THAT...
SORE SUBJECT, RIGHT, BUDDY? HEH-HEH...
GRUMBLE...
NUDGE!

...SO WHAT ARE YOU CRAWLING AROUND THESE WOODS FOR AT SEVEN O'CLOCK IN THE MORNING? ARE YOU LOST OR SOME-THING?
SURE LOOKS THAT WAY, DOESN'T IT? HEH-HEH...

SAY, YOU GOT ANY UN-OPENED BEERS LEFT? I'M PARCHED...
HERE'S ONE. IT FEELS PRETTY WARM, THOUGH...

THAT'S OKAY. I PREFER 'EM THAT WAY.
SPROCK!

GLUG! GLUG! GLUG!

...AHHHHH! THE PAUSE THAT REFRESHES...
WE'RE STILL WAITING TO HEAR YOUR STORY, JOEL...

OH YEAH... (BURP!)
WELL, WHAT HAPPENED WAS ME AND SOME BUDDIES OF MINE WENT HUNTING YESTERDAY — DIDN'T CATCH SHIT, BY THE WAY...
...AND BY NIGHTFALL WE PROCEEDED TO PARTY OUR ASSES OFF...
TOSS!

...I WANDERED OFF BY MYSELF AT SOME POINT AND COULDN'T FIND MY WAY BACK. END OF STORY.
THAT'S THE LAST TIME I'LL TAKE ECSTASY ON A HUNTING TRIP... HEH-HEH...

YOU WANDERED THROUGH THE WOODS ALL NIGHT WHILE HIGH ON "ECSTACY"?

UH-HUH... IT WAS GREAT, ACTUALLY!
HERE, YA WANT SOME?
OH! I, UH... (OKAY!)

—HEY, YOU REALLY ARE A RED HEAD, AREN'T YOU?
HUH? WELL, YEAH! WHY?

BECAUSE THE HAIR ON YOUR LEGS ARE THE SAME COLOR...
DOES THIS MEAN YOU'VE GOT RED PUBES AS WELL?
?!? UH, WELL, YEAH, A SORTOFA DARKISH RED...

REALLY? WOW! THAT'S, LIKE, A TOTAL TURN ON FOR ME!
BLUSH!
HEY JOEL, I'LL BE HAPPY TO GIVE YOU A RIDE BACK TO CIVILIZATION IF YOU'LL HELP ME WITH ALL OF THIS STUFF...

—HUH? OH, SURE! THANKS!
LET'S GET A MOVE ON, THEN...

...(IT'D BE MUCH EASIER TO HATE THIS GUY WITH TOTAL IMPUNITY IF ONLY HE WASN'T SO STUPID)...
...IF YA WANNA GET TO HEAVEN... YA GOTTA RAISE A LITTLE HELL...

DAYS LATER...
...WHO WAS THAT ON THE PHONE?
YOUR AUNT FRIEDA. SHE'S GOING TO BE STAYING WITH US FOR A FEW DAYS NEXT WEEK...
CLICK!

AUNT FRIEDA? I THOUGHT YOU HATED AUNT FRIEDA!
YOUR FATHER HATED HER. I NEVER MINDED HER TOO MUCH, THOUGH SHE CAN BE DIFFICULT AT TIMES...

OH, I SEE...
...SO AS SOON AS THE OLD MAN DIES WE BECOME A WAY STATION FOR EVERY OBNOXIOUS RELATIVE IN A THOUSAND MILE RADIUS...
BUDDY! THAT'S NO WAY TO TALK ABOUT FAMILY!
CHOMP!

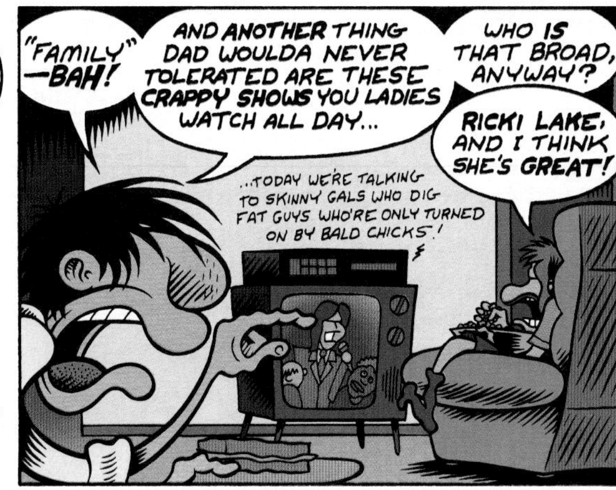
"FAMILY" —BAH!
AND ANOTHER THING DAD WOULDA NEVER TOLERATED ARE THESE CRAPPY SHOWS YOU LADIES WATCH ALL DAY...
WHO IS THAT BROAD, ANYWAY?
RICKI LAKE, AND I THINK SHE'S GREAT!
...TODAY WE'RE TALKING TO SKINNY GALS WHO DIG FAT GUYS WHO'RE ONLY TURNED ON BY BALD CHICKS!

BAH! JUST LOOK AT HER EXPRESSION— LIKE THE CAT THAT ATE THE CANARY...
SHE'S DOCUMENTING THE DOWNFALL OF WESTERN CIVILIZATION AND SHE THINKS IT'S CUTE!
AND YOU SOUND LIKE YOU'VE BEEN WATCHING TOO MUCH PAT ROBERTSON...
...WHY CAN'T SOCIETY JUST LET THEM DO THEIR OWN THING? <APPLAUSE!<

OH YEAH, RIGHT... AS FAR AS I'M CONCERNED SHE AND PAT ROBERTSON ARE TWO SIDES OF THE SAME COIN...
?!? WHAT ARE YOU TALKING ABOUT?
...THEY SHOULD COMBINE FORCES AND CALL THEIR SHOW "APOCALYPSE-A-GO-GO"...

BRUMMBRUMMBRM...
?!?
WHAT'S MAKING THAT RACKET?
BEATS ME. I'LL GO TAKE A LOOK...

....OH NO! IT'S JOEL IN HIS NEW HOT ROD!
WHAT THE HELL IS HE DOING HERE?
RUMBLE...
TRANS AM
DEATH
RUMBLE...

I HAVE NO IDEA WHY HE'S HERE...
I CERTAINLY DIDN'T INVITE HIM, IF THAT'S WHAT YOU'RE THINKING...
J-J-JOEL? Y-YOU MEAN BABS' EX-HUSBAND, JOEL?
WHO ELSE?

...BOY OH BOY, TALK ABOUT YOUR PROVERBIAL BARBARIANS AT THE GATE...
NOW THAT THE OLD MAN'S GONE HE ASSUMES THAT THIS IS SAFE TERRITORY ONCE AGAIN...
SLAM!

...YOU'RE NOT GONNA LET HIM IN, ARE YA, MA?
WELL, NOW, BUDDY, HE IS THE FATHER OF YOUR NIECE AND NEPHEW, AFTER ALL...

PHOOEY! WHY DON'T YOU ASK HIM HOW MANY CHILD SUPPORT PAYMENTS HIS NEW CAR COST HIM!
OR BETTER YET I'LL ASK HIM MY-SELF...
DON'T YOU DARE! I DON'T NEED ANY UGLY CONFRONTATIONS AROUND HERE!

BESIDES, THAT'S FOR HIM AND BABS TO WORK OUT...
OR HIM AND BABS' LAWYER, IF ONLY SHE'D HIRE ONE...
DING! DONG!
NOW EXCUSE ME WHILE I GO HIDE IN MY ROOM.

—HEY, MRS. B! LONG TIME NO SEE!
HELLO, JOEL. C'MON IN.

...AND GEE, I'M TERRIBLY SORRY TO HEAR ABOUT MR. B...
I WOULDA GONE TO THE FUNERAL, BUT, WELL, YOU KNOW HOW IT IS...
THAT'S OKAY, JOEL. I UNDERSTAND...
AND, UH, THAT'S QUITE A NEW CAR YOU GOT THERE, BY THE WAY...

YA LIKE IT?
OH, IT'S ACTUALLY OVER FIFTEEN YEARS OLD, AND IT NEEDS A LOT OF WORK, SO I HOPE YOU DON'T THINK I'M BEING EXTRAVAGANT...
UH-HUH...

IN FACT, I WAS THINKING OF THE KIDS WHEN I BOUGHT IT, SINCE I COULDN'T FIT THE TWO OF THEM ON MY MOTOR-CYCLE...
THIS IS MUCH MORE PRACTICAL, DON'T YOU THINK?
I'M SURE THE KIDS'LL LOVE IT...
WOULD YOU LIKE SOME COFFEE?

NAH. I JUST WANTED TO SHOW BUDDY MY NEW SET OF WHEELS...
...IS HE HOME?
BUDDY? I, UH...

...I FIGURED BUDDY'D LOVE TO TAKE IT FOR A TEST SPIN, 'CUZ HE AND I USED TO REALLY LUST AFTER TRANS AMS BACK IN OUR HIGH SCHOOL DAYS...
I NEVER LUSTED AFTER NO GODDAMN TRANS AM!
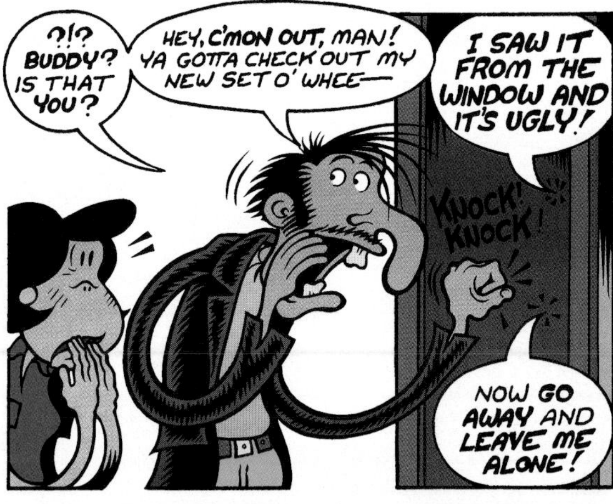
?!? BUDDY? IS THAT YOU?
HEY, C'MON OUT, MAN! YA GOTTA CHECK OUT MY NEW SET O' WHEE—
I SAW IT FROM THE WINDOW AND IT'S UGLY!
KNOCK! KNOCK!
NOW GO AWAY AND LEAVE ME ALONE!

HUH! WELL, EXCUSE ME! I JUST FIGURED THAT—
I'D LIKE TO SEE IT, JOEL.

HUH?
OH, HIYA, RED! HOWZIT GOIN'?
GOT TIME FOR A LITTLE SPIN?
I, UH... SURE!

WELL, ALRIGHT!
LET'S GO!
!
?

...HOW MUCH DO YOU KNOW ABOUT CARS?
N-NOT MUCH...
TRANS AM
STUD

OH NO?
WELL, HOP IN ANYWAY, 'CUZ YOU'RE IN FOR A BIG THRILL...
OH YEAH?
TRANS AM
STUD
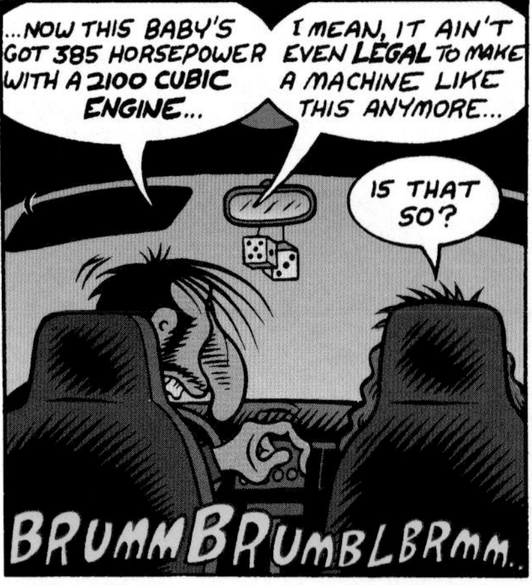
...NOW THIS BABY'S GOT 385 HORSEPOWER WITH A 2100 CUBIC ENGINE...
I MEAN, IT AIN'T EVEN LEGAL TO MAKE A MACHINE LIKE THIS ANYMORE...
IS THAT SO?
BRUMMBRUMBLBRMM.

YEP! NOW JUST LISTEN TO THIS!
VROOOM!

HOW ABOUT THAT! CAN YOU FEEL THAT POWER OR WHAT?
UH-HUH...
OMIGOD! I'M HAVING AN ORGASM!

LATER, AT "B+J'S COLLECTOR'S EMPORIUM"...

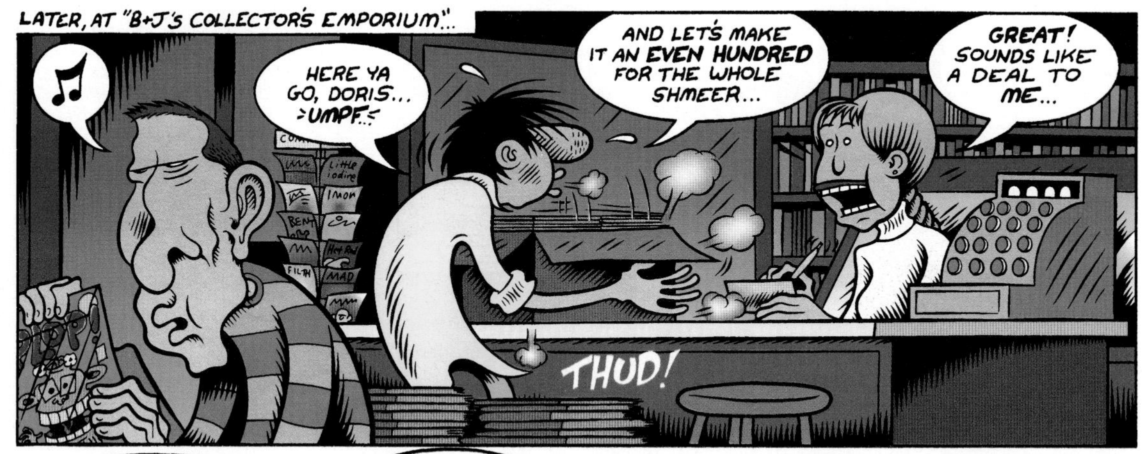

BECAUSE I FEEL SO... I DUNNO... SEXLESS LATELY...
"SEXLESS"?

YEAH, YOU KNOW, LIKE I HAVE NO SEX DRIVE LEFT...
IT'S LIKE SEX JUST DOESN'T SEEM LIKE THAT BIG A DEAL TO ME ANYMORE FOR SOME REASON...
HMMM...

HAVE YOU EVER FELT THIS WAY?
UH, ONLY WHEN IT'S BEEN CHEMICALLY INDUCED...
OTHERWISE NO—IF ANYTHING I'VE BEEN GETTING HORNIER AS I GET OLDER!

:SIGH: OH WELL... MAYBE THERE'S SOMETHING WRONG WITH ME...
MAYBE I SHOULD SEE A DOCTOR OR SOMETHING...
OR MAYBE YOU'RE JUST FULL OF CRAP...

HUH? WHADAYA MEAN BY THAT REMARK?
HEY, I SAW YOU CHECKING OUT DORIS'S ASS RIGHT BEFORE YOU STARTED IN ON THIS "WOE IS ME, I HAVE NO SEX DRIVE" ROUTINE...

AND YOU WERE FLIRTING WITH HER PRETTY SHAMELESSLY BEFORE THAT, TOO...
IT WAS MAKING ME NAUSEOUS...
:GULP!:
COMIC
LITTLE IODINE
CRACK

OH MAN, WAS I THAT OBVIOUS?
SHIT... HOW EMBARRASSING...

I CAN'T HELP IT, THOUGH! SHE'S SO SWEET AND HEALTHY AND WELL-ADJUSTED!
SHE'S THE EXACT OPPOSITE OF —UHHH...
UH-OH...

UH... NEVER MIND... FORGET I SAID ANYTHING...
TROUBLE IN PARADISE BETWEEN YOU AND LISA, I GATHER?

OH, IT'S NOTHING, OTHER THAN THE FACT THAT MY WORST FEARS HAVE COME TRUE...
THE INSTANT MY FATHER DIED SHE TURNED INTO A DIFFERENT PERSON: COLD, DISTANT, HUMORLESS...
NO SEX EITHER, HUH?
SICK
ANGEL

UH, YEAH... THAT TOO...
:SIGH:...OH WELL, ALL I CAN SUGGEST IS THAT YOU HANG TIGHT AND RIDE IT OUT...
PAT PAT

...OF COURSE, IF MY GIRLFRIEND EVER HELD OUT ON ME I'D DUMP THE BITCH IN AN INSTANT, BUT THAT'S THE ADVICE I ALWAYS GIVE MY FRIENDS: JUST RIDE IT OUT...
GEE, THANKS...

THE FOLLOWING SATURDAY MORNING...

...EXCUSE ME, MS. LEAVENWORTH, BUT CAN YOU TELL ME WHY IT IS THAT YOU'RE ALWAYS EXACTLY TWENTY MINUTES LATE?
S-SORRY. I, UH...
HEY, DOES THIS STORE HAVE "POCAHONTAS" ON VIDEO YET?

NEVER MIND. JUST PUT THESE RETURNS BACK ON THE SHELVES.
=AHEM= I SAID, IS "POCAHONTAS" OUT ON VIDEO YET!
HMM? NO, NOT YET. TWO WEEKS.

HEY, LADY! DO YOU HAVE "POCAHONTAS" YET?
NO, NOT YET. SOON.

NO POCAHONTAS? GODDAMMIT TO HELL!!
= SIGH = ISN'T ANY-ONE INTERESTED IN ANY OF OUR 10,000 OTHER MOVIES?

PARDON ME, MA'AM...
WHAT IS IT?
DON'T SAY IT, MISTER!

...(ER, UH, WHERE IS YOUR "ADULT" SECTION?)
OH! IT'S RIGHT OVER THERE, SIR, BEHIND THAT DOOR...

THANK YOU...
DON'T MENTION IT!

—OH, AND BY THE WAY, HAS "POCAHONTAS" COME OUT ON VIDEO YET?

LATER...
YES, YOU CAN TAKE YOUR LUNCH BREAK NOW, LISA.

IQUE SHOE
PHO

FLIP! FLIP!

TEN MINUTES LATER...

THAT'LL DO...
PUSH!
?!?

YANK!
=GASP!=

ZZZZIP!
SHLORCK!
UNGH! OMIGOD...

WHAM! BAM! SLAM!
OOH! OOH! OOH!
UGH! UGH! UGH!

OOMPF! OOMPF! OOMPF!
WANKA! WANKA! WANKA!

WHOO! WHOO! WHOO!
BOINGA! BOINGA! SPROINGA!

UMPF! UMPF! SLUMPF!
MUNCH! SLOBBER! CHEW!

15 MINUTES LATER...
...UGGHHHHHH...

—OH MY GOSH! LOOK AT THE TIME!
?

I'VE GOTTA HUSTLE OR I'LL BE LATE FOR WORK AGAIN...
B-BUT, YOU JUST GOT HERE! CAN'T YA STICK AROUND FOR A LITTLE WHILE?
SPROING!

NUH-UH, SORRY. MY BOSS IS PISSED OFF ENOUGH AS IT IS...
WHERE'S MY PURSE?
WELL, GEE, WE HARDLY EVEN TALKED OR HUNG OUT OR ANY-THING...

WHEN WILL I SEE YOU AGAIN?
I DUNNO. I'LL CALL YA...
BYE!

...I SHOULD MAKE IT BACK ON TIME...

PHONE PHONE
PETS
TOYS
SCREEECH!

RING! RING! R—
—HELLO?

IF YOU TELL ANYONE ABOUT WHAT JUST HAPPENED I SWEAR TO GOD I'LL KILL YOU!!!

THE NEXT DAY...

C'MON, LISA. IF WE'RE GONNA GET TO THE TRADE SHOW ON TIME I COULD REALLY USE YOUR HELP...
I'M NOT GOING.
TV GUIDE

HUH? WHADAYA MEAN, YOU'RE NOT GOING?
I JUST DON'T FEEL LIKE GOING, THAT'S ALL...
WHAT DO YOU NEED ME FOR, ANYWAY...
CLICK!

WE DON'T NEED YOU! BUT YOU KEPT TELLING ME ALL WEEK HOW YOU WANTED TO COME ALONG, AND NOW ALL OF A SUDDEN YOU—
OH, LEAVE HER ALONE, BUDDY! SHE WANTS TO STAY HERE, SO CAN WE PLEASE DROP THE SUBJECT?
YEAH!

=SIGH= FINE, SUIT YOURSELF... MUTTER FUME...
HEY, LISA, HOW'D YOU LIKE TO DO SOMETHING WITH ME 'N' THE KIDS TODAY?
...JOEL SHOULD BE BRINGIN' 'EM BY ANY MINUTE—
WHAT? DID YOU SAY JOEL?

—YEAH, CAN YOU BELIEVE IT? HE'S ACTUALLY BEEN PRETTY GOOD WITH THE KIDS LATELY...
RING! RING!
DRAT. THERE'S THE PHONE...
...(UH, BUDDY, MAYBE I WILL GO WITH YOU AFTER ALL)...
?!? ARE YOU SERIOUS?

(OH, I GET IT. YOU JUST DON'T WANT TO BE AROUND WHEN MY SISTER'S BRATTY KIDS SHOW UP, IS THAT IT?)
(ER, UH, YEAH, THAT'S THE REASON ALL RIGHT)...
OH BABS, JOEL'S ON THE PHONE...
OH, GREAT. NOW WHAT?

WELL, YOU MIGHT AS WELL MAKE YOURSELF USEFUL BY HELPING ME LOAD UP THE TRUCK...
SURE, FINE. LET'S JUST HURRY UP AND GET OUT OF HERE...
...OH BUDDY! IS THIS SWAP MEET THINGY YOU'RE GOING TO A GOOD PLACE TO BRING KIDS?

HMM? WELL, YEAH, I'M SURE THEY'LL GET A KICK OUT OF IT, SINCE IT'S BASICALLY A TOY COLLECTOR'S CONVENTION...
GREAT!
—SURE, JOEL, YOU CAN BRING THE KIDS THERE, THOUGH THEY'LL PROBABLY EXPECT YOU TO BUY THEM SOMETHING...

SO JOEL'S BRINGING THE KIDS TO THE SHOW, HUH?
...OOF!
YES, THANK GOD! IT GIVES ME A FEW MORE PRECIOUS HOURS TO BE BY MY-SELF...
CLICK!
UH, I DON'T THINK I'LL BE GOING AFTER ALL, BUDDY...

WHAT?!
I-I DON'T FEEL SO GOOD...
NOW IF YOU'LL EXCUSE ME...
?

WHAT'S WRONG WITH LISA?
IS SHE OKAY?
YOU'RE ASKING ME? I DON'T HAVE A CLUE!

WELL, WHY DON'T YOU GO CHECK UP ON HER AND FIND OUT?
YEAH, FOR ALL YOU KNOW SHE MIGHT BE REALLY SICK!
ARRRGH...

KNOCK! KNOCK!
...LISA? ARE YOU OKAY?
GO AWAY AND LEAVE ME ALONE!
BLARF!

SERIOUSLY, LISA, I—
I SAID GO AWAY! AND DON'T TOUCH ME!
EVERY TIME YOU TOUCH ME IT MAKES MY SKIN CRAWL!

?!? OH REALLY! WELL, THAT'S JUST GREAT! I'M GLAD TO SEE IT'S COME TO THIS!
OHHHHHHH... PLEASE BE QUIET...
RETCH!

I WON'T BE QUIET! FIRST THING TOMORROW I'M GONNA MAKE AN APPOINT-MENT FOR YOU TO SEE A SHRINK!
UNLESS YOU'D RATHER I NOT EVER TOUCH YOU AGAIN, THAT IS!
HACK
SPIT
KOFF

MEANWHILE, I HAVE SOME TAWDRY, OVERPRICED PIECES OF MEMORABILIA TO UNLOAD...
GOOD DAY, MS. LEAVENWORTH!
BLORF!
?

...WHOA, YOU LOOK **PRETTY BURNED OUT** THIS MORNING, BUDDY. DIDN'T YOU GET ENOUGH SLEEP LAST NIGHT?

I'M ALRIGHT... I'D REALLY RATHER NOT TALK ABOUT IT, IF YOU DON'T MIND...

MID-COUNTY COMMUNITY CENTER
MAY 18-19 TOY COLLECTORS CONVENTION
MAY 25-26-CAMP FIRE GIRLS
JUNE 3-SPORTS BANQUET
JUNE 10-
JUNE 17-18 – BASEBALL MEMORABILIA EXPO

WELCOME COLLECTORS OF 1960s-'70s MEMORABILIA!

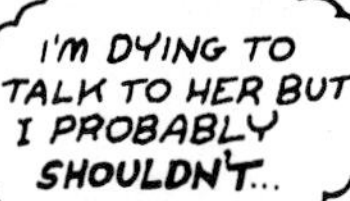

IT'S PROBABLY JUST FROM KEEPING UP WITH THE HIGH VOLUME OF BUSINESS AT THIS HAPPENIN' CON THAT'S GETTING TO ME... HEH-HEH...

YEAH, RIGHT. TELL ME ANOTHER ONE.

...LOOK, I CAN TELL SOMETHING'S **BOTHERING YOU**, BUT IF YOU THINK I'M BEIN' **NOSY** I'LL JUST—
NO— I MEAN, I DON'T MIND YOUR BEIN' **NOSY**...
FLICK!

...THE TRUTH IS THAT I'M EXPERIENCING YER TYPICAL **"RELATIONSHIP PROBLEMS"** WITH MY GIRLFRIEND **LISA** RIGHT NOW...
LIKE, WHAT **ELSE** IS NEW, RIGHT?
OH... I'M **SORRY**...

...SO, DOES THIS MEAN THE TWO OF YOU ARE, LIKE... **PFFT**?
AAH, **WHO KNOWS**...

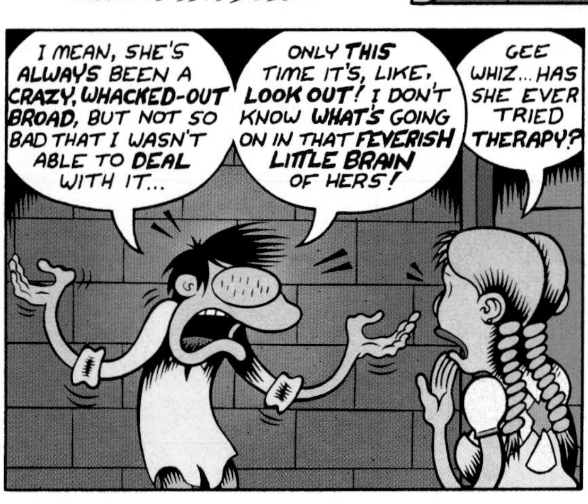
I MEAN, SHE'S **ALWAYS** BEEN A **CRAZY, WHACKED-OUT BROAD**, BUT NOT SO BAD THAT I WASN'T ABLE TO **DEAL** WITH IT...
ONLY **THIS** TIME IT'S, LIKE, **LOOK OUT**! I DON'T KNOW **WHAT'S** GOING ON IN THAT **FEVERISH LITTLE BRAIN** OF HERS!
GEE WHIZ... HAS SHE EVER TRIED **THERAPY**?

NOT AS LONG AS **I'VE** KNOWN HER...
SHE'S CONVINCED THAT IF SHE TOLD SOME SHRINK THE **WHOLE TRUTH** THAT HE'D HAVE HER **LOCKED UP**...
=**TSK**!= OH, THAT'S **SILLY**...

I DUNNO... SHE MAY ACTUALLY HAVE A **POINT** THERE...
WELL, MAYBE YOU SHOULD **BOTH** SEE A COUNSELOR, BECAUSE IT WOULD BE A SHAME TO JUST LET IT END AFTER **ALL THESE YEARS**...

I THINK PEOPLE ARE **WAY** TOO QUICK TO **GIVE UP** ON EACH OTHER THESE DAYS...
YA GOTTA **HANG IN THERE** AND MAKE IT **WORK**!
HMMM...

SO I SHOULD "RIDE IT OUT", IS **THAT** WHAT YOU'RE SAYIN'?
WELL, **YEAH**! I MEAN, THAT'S WHAT **LOVE'S ALL ABOUT**, RIGHT?

OH YEAH... **"LOVE"**... HOW COULD **I FORGET**...
=**TSK**!= OH YOU...

C'MERE, YOU, AND GIMME A **BIG HUG**!
THINGS AREN'T **SO** BAD!
STOP BEIN' SUCH A **GLOOMY GUS**!
?!?

I SHOULD BE GETTING BACK TO MY TABLE NOW, BUT YOU **TAKE CARE OF YOURSELF**, OKAY?

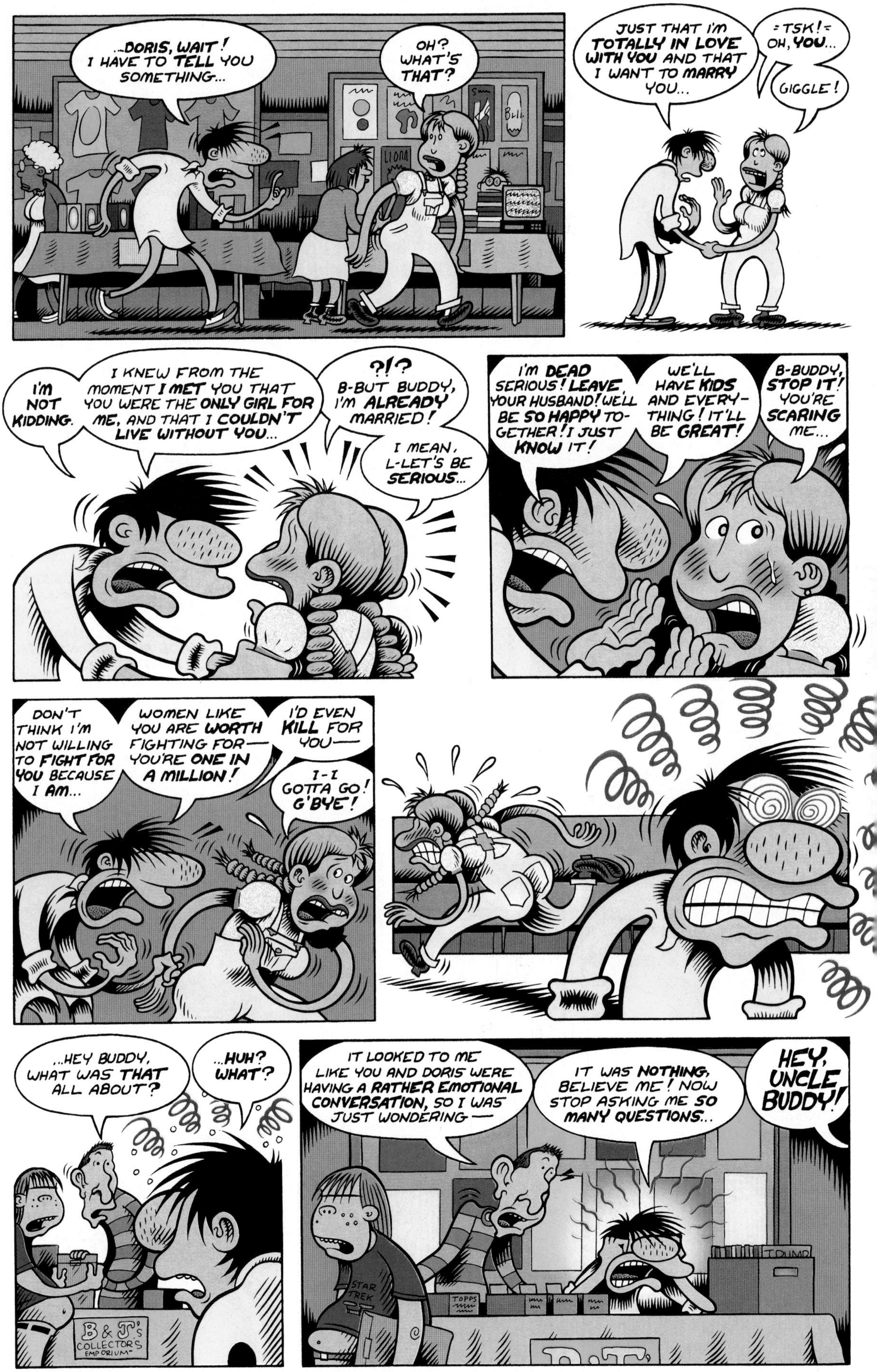

...DORIS, WAIT! I HAVE TO TELL YOU SOMETHING...

OH? WHAT'S THAT?

JUST THAT I'M TOTALLY IN LOVE WITH YOU AND THAT I WANT TO MARRY YOU...

=TSK!= OH, YOU...

GIGGLE!

I'M NOT KIDDING.

I KNEW FROM THE MOMENT I MET YOU THAT YOU WERE THE ONLY GIRL FOR ME, AND THAT I COULDN'T LIVE WITHOUT YOU...

?!? B-BUT BUDDY, I'M ALREADY MARRIED!

I MEAN, L-LET'S BE SERIOUS...

I'M DEAD SERIOUS! LEAVE YOUR HUSBAND! WE'LL BE SO HAPPY TOGETHER! I JUST KNOW IT!

WE'LL HAVE KIDS AND EVERYTHING! IT'LL BE GREAT!

B-BUDDY, STOP IT! YOU'RE SCARING ME...

DON'T THINK I'M NOT WILLING TO FIGHT FOR YOU BECAUSE I AM...

WOMEN LIKE YOU ARE WORTH FIGHTING FOR— YOU'RE ONE IN A MILLION!

I'D EVEN KILL FOR YOU—

I-I GOTTA GO! G'BYE!

—HUH? OH, GOOD GRIEF...
THIS PLACE IS GREAT!
YEAH! LOOK AT ALL THIS COOL STUFF WE BOUGHT!
HI, UH... JAY, RIGHT?
HOWZIT GOIN', JOEL...
LOOK WHAT I GOT, UNCLE BUDDY! IT'S A BUTTERFLY PRINCESS BARBIE!
AND I GOT THIS FAKE KNIFE!
TAKE THAT!
OW!

TYLER, THAT HURT!
GET AWAY FROM ME WITH THAT THING!
SO, HOW'S BUSINESS BEEN FOR YOU GUYS TODAY?
SORRY...

BUSINESS SUCKS!
WHAT'S IT TO YOU, ANY-WAY?
W-WELL GEE, I WAS JUST ASKIN'!

YOU THINK JUST 'CUZ YOU TAKE THE KIDS FOR A DAY AND SPEND MONEY ON 'EM THAT YOU DESERVE AN AWARD OR SOMETHING?
YOU'RE STILL A NO-GOOD DEADBEAT AS FAR AS I'M CONCERNED!
JESUS, BUDDY...
HEY. THESE BASEBALL CARDS ALL HAVE NAKED LADIES ON 'EM!

GET AWAY FROM THOSE, YA LITTLE PERV! THEY'RE NOT FOR KIDS!
...L-L-LISA TOLD YOU, DIDN'T SHE...
BUT—
SNATCH!

...HUH? TOLD ME WHAT?
OH, UH, NOTHING! NEVER MIND!

C-C'MON, KIDS, WE OUGHT TO BE GOING...
FINE WITH ME! UNCLE BUDDY'S CRANKY TODAY!
YEAH, AND HE SELLS THE WORST STUFF!
GOOD RIDDANCE!

..?!? WHAT'RE YOU LOOKIN' AT? WHAT'S YOUR PROBLEM?
I WAS JUST ABOUT TO ASK YOU THE SAME QUESTION...

WHO, ME? NOTHIN', 'CEPT FOR THE FACT THAT MY LIFE'S A TOTAL JOKE, IS ALL...
THAT AND THE FACT THAT YOU'RE A TOTAL ASSHOLE...

...YEAH... THAT TOO...

LATE THAT NIGHT...
BRUMBLBRUMBLM
THE BRADLEYS

WAHOO!
THE BRADLEYS
SMASH!

SCREEECH!

AHHHH... HOME AT LAST...
...HOME SWEET HOME...
:HIC:

SPLAT!

BUDDY, IS THAT YOU? WHAT ON EARTH ARE YOU DOING!?
GROANNN...

AND IS LISA WITH YOU? I WANT THE TWO OF YOU IN THE HOUSE THIS INSTANT BEFORE YOU WAKE UP THE WHOLE NEIGHBORHOOD...
LISA?

YOU'RE ASKING ME WHERE LISA IS? ISN'T SHE SUPPOSED TO BE SICK IN BED?
OH... I DUNNO...
SHE MAY BE, I DIDN'T CHECK...

BUT COME INSIDE ANYWAY BEFORE YOU CATCH PNEUMO-NIA...
YOU LOOK LIKE A DRUNKEN FOOL LYING OUT THERE...
I AM A DRUNKEN FOOL...
AND I HAPPEN TO LIKE IT HERE IN THE GREAT OUTDOORS...

—HEY MA, HAVE YOU EVER "DONE IT" IN THE GREAT OUTDOORS? 'CUZ I SURE HAVEN'T...
HAVE I EVER—? OH, FER CRYIN'—

GOODNIGHT, BUDDY!
SLAM!
...I WONDER IF LISA'S "DOIN' IT" IN THE GREAT OUTDOORS RIGHT NOW...
ZZZZz...

NEXT MORNING....

...OKAY, WHAT?
ALL RIGHT, NOW LISTEN TO ME CAREFULLY, YOU TWO...

...DON'T THINK I HAVEN'T NOTICED THAT THINGS HAVEN'T EXACTLY BEEN THE SAME SINCE DAD DIED...
WE'RE ALL GOING THROUGH A PERIOD OF RE-ADJUSTMENT, AND IT HASN'T BEEN EASY FOR ANY OF US...
GROANNN... THAT'S JUST THE TIP OF THE ICEBERG...

OKAY, SO MAYBE I DON'T KNOW EVERYTHING THAT'S GOING ON BETWEEN THE TWO OF YOU, AND I DON'T WANT TO KNOW...
WHAT I DO KNOW IS THAT IF YOU CAN'T AT LEAST ACT NICER TO EACH OTHER THEN YOU'LL HAVE TO FIND ANOTHER PLACE TO LIVE, 'CUZ I CAN'T TAKE ALL OF THIS NASTINESS ANYMORE!
BUT IT AIN'T JUST A MATTER OF BEING NICE, MA...

...I ALWAYS TRY TO BE NICE TO LISA, BUT HOW AM I SUPPOSED TO DEAL WITH SOMEONE WHO'S TOTALLY IRRATIONAL? EVER SINCE DAD DIED—
WHADAYA MEAN, I'M "IRRATIONAL"? HOW AM I SUPPOSED TO BEHAVE? WHAT THE HELL DO YOU WANT FROM ME?!
OH GOD, HERE WE GO...

WHAT DO I WANT? WHAT DO YOU MEAN, "WHAT DO I WANT?" WHAT DO I THINK I WANT?
I MEAN BESIDES SEX! AND DON'T BE VAGUE, BECAUSE—
=SOB=

?!? WHAT ARE YOU CRYING ABOUT, MOM?
?
?!? WHAT AM I CRYING ABOUT?

I'M CRYING BECAUSE MY HUSBAND'S DEAD AND I MISS HIM!
WHAT DO YOU THINK I'M CRYING ABOUT?

=BOO-HOO-HOO-HOO-HOO=.

SLAM!

...BOY, DO I FEEL LIKE A HEEL...
DON'T FEEL TOO BAD... I HAD NO IDEA WHY SHE WAS CRYING EITHER...

THAT NIGHT...
...UGH, UGH, UGH, UGH...

UNNGH!

...AHHHHH... I FEEL LIKE I JUST UNLOADED A GALLON OF CUM IN YOU...
AWWW... IT WAS PRETTY BACKED-UP IN THERE, HUH?
UH-HUH...
PAT, PAT...

...BUDDY?
UMM?

HOW COME YOU DON'T POUND AWAY AT ME LIKE YOU USED TO?
?!? "POUND AWAY"?

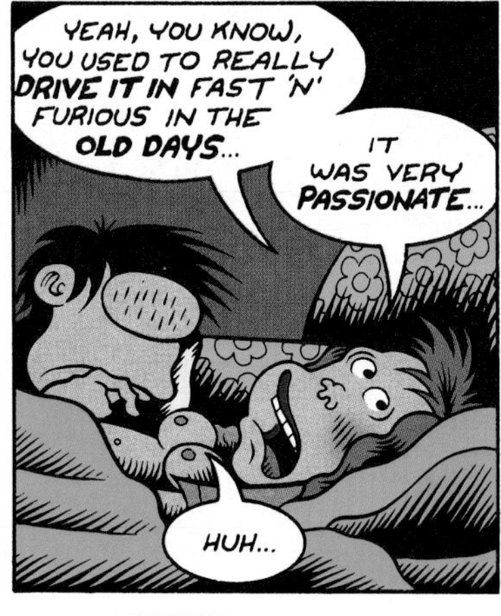
YEAH, YOU KNOW, YOU USED TO REALLY DRIVE IT IN FAST 'N' FURIOUS IN THE OLD DAYS...
IT WAS VERY PASSIONATE...
HUH...

I THINK THAT HAD LESS TO DO WITH PASSION THAN WITH A SIMPLE LACK OF CONTROL...
BESIDES, YOU USED TO COMPLAIN WHEN I'D DO THAT...
I DID?

UH-HUH. BECAUSE YOU WEREN'T GETTING ENOUGH "CLIT-FRICTION" OR SOMETHING...
OH, YEAH. I GUESS THAT'S TRUE...

BUT I'LL "POUND AWAY" NEXT TIME IF YOU WANT ME TO...
NAH, THAT'S OKAY...

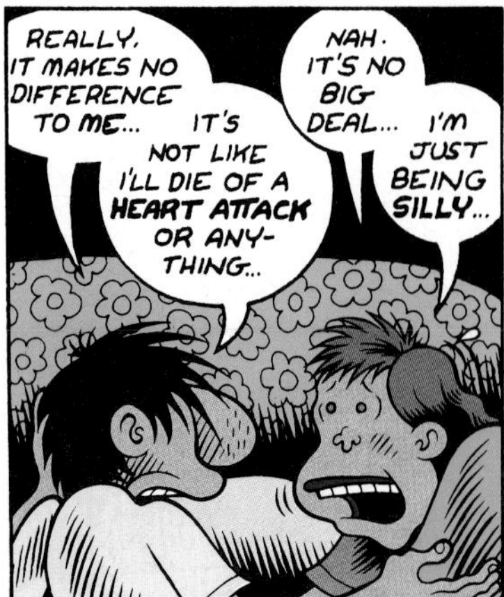
REALLY, IT MAKES NO DIFFERENCE TO ME... IT'S NOT LIKE I'LL DIE OF A HEART ATTACK OR ANY-THING...
NAH. IT'S NO BIG DEAL... I'M JUST BEING SILLY...

SUIT YERSELF...
G'NIGHT, LISA...
G'NIGHT...

BESIDES, IF I'M EVER IN THE MOOD FOR A "POUNDING" I'LL JUST CALL JOEL, 'CUZ HE'S BETTER AT IT!
ZZZZzz...
END.

BUDDY BRADLEY
AND THE LOVELY
LISA LEAVENWORTH
in
BUDDY
LISA
"...NOTHING THAT TWENTY YEARS ON THE COUCH COULDN'T CURE!"
©1996 BY PETER BAGGE
ART BY P. BAGGE AND
JIM BLANCHARD
...EEEYOW! WHAT THE HELL'D YA DO THAT FOR?!?
THAT'S FOR IGNORING ME, YA BIG...BIG... JERKER-OFFER!

"IGNORING YOU"? HOW COULD I BE IGNORING YOU WHEN WE WEREN'T EVEN IN THE SAME ROOM 'TIL NOW?
THAT'S JUST IT! AND YOU DIDN'T EVEN NOTICE THAT I LEFT THE HOUSE FOR A WHOLE HOUR!
YOU JUST SAT DOWN HERE BY YOURSELF— MASTURBATING!

WHA?! SAY, NOW WAIT A MINUTE...
THE LAST TIME I SAW YOU YOU SITTING UPSTAIRS SIPPING COFFEE AND WATCHING JEOPARDY...
THAT'S RIGHT! AND THAT WAS OVER TWO HOURS AGO!

RIGHT! AND I ASKED YOU IF I WANTED TO DO SOMETHING LIKE PLAY SCRABBLE WITH ME AND YOU SAID NO!
...SHIT, LOOK AT THIS MESS...
THAT'S RIGHT! AND THEN YOU JUST TURNED AROUND AND WALKED AWAY, WHICH TOLD ME THAT YOU DIDN'T REALLY WANT TO BE WITH ME AT ALL—THAT YOU WERE JUST SAYING THAT!
SQUEEZE!

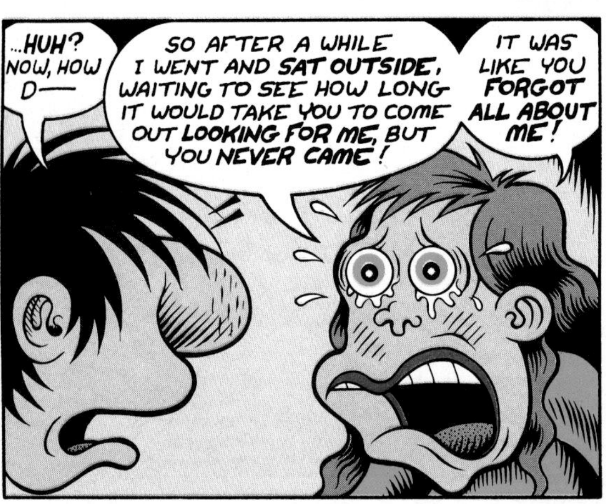
...HUH? NOW, HOW D—
SO AFTER A WHILE I WENT AND SAT OUTSIDE, WAITING TO SEE HOW LONG IT WOULD TAKE YOU TO COME OUT LOOKING FOR ME, BUT YOU NEVER CAME!
IT WAS LIKE YOU FORGOT ALL ABOUT ME!

HOLY SMOKES... I CAN'T BELIEVE MY EARS...
...SO THEN I PEEKED THROUGH THE WINDOW TO SEE WHAT YOU WERE UP TO, AND THAT'S WHEN I CAUGHT YOU READING THIS VILE PORNOGRAPHY WHILE YOU PLAYED WITH YOUR RAGING HARD-ON!
Tease!

HA! I WISH! IT'S BEEN YEARS SINCE I HAD A "RAGING HARD-ON"...
I WAS JUST SCRATCHING MY NUTS THE WAY I ALWAYS DO WHEN I'M SITTING AROUND IN MY UNDERWEAR...
>SNIFF< ...DO YOU WISH I LOOKED LIKE THIS?
Tease

LIKE WHAT, AN ILLUSTRATION FROM THE 1940s? NO, I WISH I LOOKED LIKE THAT...
GIMME A BREAK, LISA!!!... I MEAN, JEEZ...
>SNIFF!<

-UMPF!
FLING!
HEY!
SPLAT!

WHAT IS IT WITH YOU TODAY, LISA? YOU'RE ALL STEAMED UP OVER NOTHING!
HOW MANY CUPS OF COFFEE HAVE YOU HAD TODAY, ANYWAY? TEN?

I'VE HAD NINE CUPS OF COFFEE, AND SO WHAT?
NINE? GEE WHIZ, NO WONDER...

MY CAFFEINE ADDICTION HAS NOTHING TO DO WITH IT!
OKAY, FINE, HAVE IT YOUR WAY...
PARANOIA

...IF YOU WANT TO INSIST THAT YOU HAVE NOTHING TO BLAME FOR YOUR IRRATIONAL BEHAVIOR OTHER THAN YOUR OWN INGRAINED INSANITY, THEN WHO AM I TO ARGUE?

— IF I'M CRAZY IT'S ONLY BECAUSE YOU'RE MAKING ME CRAZY! YOU AND YOUR STUPID ODD-BALL MAGAZINES!
?!?
GIMME THAT!
PARANOIA

GRRRRRRR...
THAT DOES IT...
STOMP! STOMP!
STOMP! STOMP!

...LISA, IF YOU DON'T MAKE AN APPOINTMENT TO SEE A SHRINK FIRST THING TOMORROW MORNING THEN WE'RE THROUGH, AND I MEAN IT THIS TIME!
?!? WHY ME? YOU'RE THE ONE WHO NEEDS HIS HEAD EXAMINED!

YOU'RE THE ONE THAT'S CRAZY, NOT ME! SO DON'T YOU THREATEN ME, YOU—
FINE, SUIT YOURSELF...

...BUT IF YOU DON'T DO WHAT I SAY THEN I'M MOVING OUT AND GETTING A PLACE OF MY OWN...
HA! THAT I'D LIKE TO SEE, MR. INDEPENDENT! MR. ALL-TALK-NO-ACTION!
YOU DON'T TELL ME WHAT TO DO, YOU NO GOOD, LOW-DOWN DIRTY BLAH, BLAH, BLAH... RANT, RAVE...

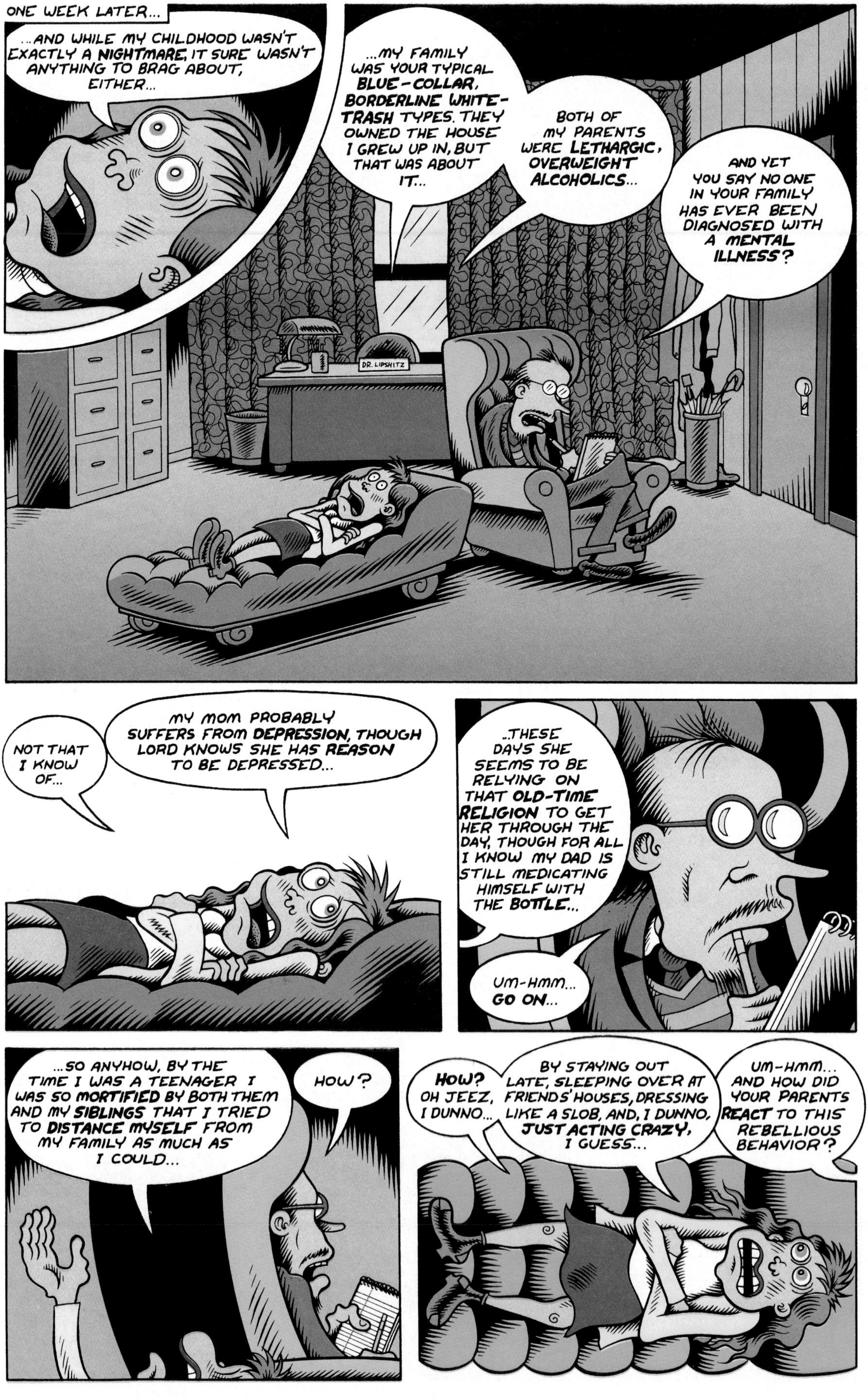

ONE WEEK LATER...

...AND WHILE MY CHILDHOOD WASN'T EXACTLY A **NIGHTMARE**, IT SURE WASN'T ANYTHING TO BRAG ABOUT, EITHER...

...MY FAMILY WAS YOUR TYPICAL **BLUE-COLLAR, BORDERLINE WHITE-TRASH** TYPES. THEY OWNED THE HOUSE I GREW UP IN, BUT THAT WAS ABOUT IT...

BOTH OF MY PARENTS WERE **LETHARGIC, OVERWEIGHT ALCOHOLICS**...

AND YET YOU SAY NO ONE IN YOUR FAMILY HAS EVER BEEN DIAGNOSED WITH A **MENTAL ILLNESS?**

DR. LIPSHITZ

NOT THAT I KNOW OF...

MY MOM PROBABLY SUFFERS FROM **DEPRESSION**, THOUGH LORD KNOWS SHE HAS **REASON** TO BE DEPRESSED...

HOW? OH JEEZ, I DUNNO...

BY STAYING OUT LATE, SLEEPING OVER AT FRIENDS' HOUSES, DRESSING LIKE A SLOB, AND, I DUNNO, **JUST ACTING CRAZY**, I GUESS...

UM-HMM... AND HOW DID YOUR PARENTS **REACT** TO THIS REBELLIOUS BEHAVIOR?

PFFT. THEY HARDLY EVEN NOTICED. GUESS THEY WERE TOO CAUGHT UP IN THEIR OWN PROBLEMS TO PAY ANY ATTENTION TO WHAT WAS UP WITH ME...
LOOKING BACK ON IT I'M AMAZED THAT THEY DIDN'T GO BALLISTIC...
WAS THAT YOUR INTENTION? TO MAKE THEM "GO BALLISTIC"?

HMM? OH JEEZ, WHO KNOWS WHAT MY INTENTIONS WERE. I SURE DIDN'T...
ALL I KNEW WAS THAT I DIDN'T WANT TO BE LIKE THEM...

...OF COURSE, I HAD NO IDEA WHAT I DID WANT OUT OF LIFE, AND I STILL DON'T... WHICH IS WHY I'M HERE, I GUESS...

BUT THEN, WHO DOES KNOW WHAT THEY WANT WHEN YOU'RE IN YOUR TEENS? ALL YOU KNOW FOR SURE IS WHAT YOU DON'T WANT — RIGHT?
MMMM, THAT MAY BE TRUE FOR SOME, BUT YOU OUGHT NOT GENERALIZE...

—OH NO? WELL, HOW ABOUT YOU? DID YOU KNOW WHAT YOU WANTED WHEN YOU WERE SIXTEEN?
ERRR, WELL, YES, BASICALLY...

IS THAT SO? AND WHAT DID YOU WANT?
TO GO TO COLLEGE, AND PURSUE A CAREER IN PSYCHIATRY...

...OH.
...I WISH WE COULD CONTINUE, BUT I'M AFRAID OUR TIME IS UP...

—REALLY? THAT WAS QUICK...
...SO NOW WHAT?
?!? I BEG YOUR PARDON?

AREN'T YOU GOING TO PRESCRIBE ME SOMETHING? LIKE PROZAC OR SOMETHING?
PROZAC? WHY, NO...
I MAY PRESCRIBE AN ANTI-DEPRESSANT ONCE—AND IF—I CONCLUDE THAT YOU DO SUFFER FROM CLINICAL DEPRESSION, BUT—

SO HOW LONG IS THAT GONNA TAKE?
I CAN'T SAY... WEEKS, MONTHS...

THAT LONG?!
SO WHAT AM I SUPPOSED TO DO IN THE MEANTIME? I STILL GOT AN ASSHOLE BOSS AND A PAIN IN THE ASS BOYFRIEND TO DEAL WITH, YA KNOW!
>SIGH<...UNLESS THEY'RE BEHAVING IN A CRIMINAL MANNER, I'D SUGGEST THAT YOU JUST TRY TO ACT AS CIVIL AS POSSIBLE 'TIL OUR NEXT VISIT...

UGH! THAT SOUNDS EXHAUSTING...
THANKS A LOT— PUTZ!
PLOP!

THAT EVENING...
BURRITO·LOCO
...AND I'M TELLIN' YA, BUTCH, SHE WOULDN'T BUDGE! IT WAS LIKE SHE WAS DEAD TO THE WORLD...
SO WHAT DID YOU DO?
SI, WE'RE OPEN

..SO I TRIED PULLING HER OUT OF BED, WHEN SHE SUDDENLY TURNS ON ME AND MAKES THIS SNARLY FACE LIKE LINDA BLAIR IN THE EXORCIST!
SCARED THE SHIT OUTTA ME, LEMME TELL YA...
JEEZUS...
SO THEN WHAT DID YOU DO?

WHAT COULD I DO? I JUST TURNED AROUND AND LEFT...
DON'T ASK ME HOW SHE GOT TO WORK ON TIME, BUT SHE MANAGED SOMEHOW...
JEE-ZUS...

I DUNNO, BUDDY...IF I WERE YOU I WOULDN'T TOLERATE SUCH ...SUCH...
SUCH WHAT, "INSUBORDINATION"? WHAT WOULD YOU SUGGEST I DO, FORCE HER OUT OF BED AND INTO HER CLOTHES?
SHE'D SCRATCH MY EYES OUT IF I EVEN TRIED...

SO? SINCE WHEN ARE YOU AFRAID OF A LITTLE CAT SCRATCH?
YOU'RE STRONGER THAN HER, AREN'T YA? IF SHE TRIES TO GET ROUGH WITH YOU THEN JUST KICK HER ASS!
OR BETTER YET KICK HER OUT!
YEAH, RIGHT...
...WAITRESS! TWO MORE, PLEASE!
SI, SEÑOR...

WHAT? HOLD ON, WAITRESS...
(BUDDY, DON'T YOU THINK YOU'VE HAD ENOUGH?)
?!? WHATEVER GAVE YOU THAT IDEA?
?

(WHEN WE CAME IN HERE YOU SAID YOU WERE GONNA JUST HAVE ONE WITH DINNER, AND YOU'VE HAD THREE ALREADY!)
SO I'VE CHANGED MY MIND! WHAT'S IT TO YOU ANYWAY?

TWO MORE, WAITRESS!
SI, SEÑOR...

LOOK, IF YOU DON'T WANT ANOTHER ONE THEN JUST SAY SO!
NO, I'M FINE... IT'S JUST THAT...
WELL...

WHAT? ARE YOU INSINUATING THAT I CAN'T HANDLE MY LIQUOR?
WELL, NOW THAT YOU MENTION IT, THERE ARE TIMES WHEN YOU TEND TO GET A LITTLE MAUDLIN...

...LIKE WHEN YOU'RE HAVING WOMEN PROBLEMS, F'RINSTANCE...
"MAUDLIN"? ME? HAH! I BET YOU DON'T EVEN KNOW WHAT THE WORD MEANS!

—AND LISTEN TO YOU! I CAN'T BELIEVE I'M GETTING ADVICE ON HOW TO HANDLE BOTH LIQUOR AND WOMEN FROM THE LIKES OF YOU!
I MEAN, CONSIDERING YOUR TRACK RECORD...
HEY, THAT'S EXACTLY WHY YOU SHOULD LISTEN TO ME —'CUZ I'VE BEEN THERE, MAN!

DON'T YOU WANT TO LEARN FROM MY MISTAKES?
BAH... THE DAY YOU LEARN FROM YOUR MISTAKES, THEN MAYBE I'LL LISTEN...

ONE HOUR LATER...
=SOB!= WHY ME?! WHY DO I ALWAYS GET STUCK WITH THE CRAZY ONES?! =BLUBBER!=
SHHH! (PULL YOURSELF TOGETHER, MAN!)

—WHAT DID I EVER DO TO DESERVE SUCH LOUSY TREATMENT!?
UHHHH, I THINK IT'S TIME TO HEAD HOME, BUDDY...

GOOD IDEA! LET'S GET OUT OF THIS DUMP!
(ER, YOU GO ON BY YOURSELF, BUDDY, WHILE I PUT THE MOVES ON THIS SAUCY MEXICAN WAITRESS...
I THINK SHE'S GOT THE HOTS FOR ME)...

...EHH? OH, YOU DO, DO YOU? I WOULDN'T BE SO SURE...
ARE YOU KIDDING? SHE'S BEEN GIVING ME "THE LOOK" ALL NIGHT!
NOW GET OUTTA HERE—YER CRAMPIN' MY STYLE!

I'M OUTTA HERE, "AMIGO", THOUGH I'D SWEAR THAT THE "LOOK" SHE WAS GIVING YOU WAS ONE OF CONTEMPT...
BUT WHAT DO I KNOW? YOU'RE THE EXPERT WHEN IT COMES TO THE OPPOSITE SEX...
AI! MUY BORRACHO!
ADIOS!
"ADIOS," "AMIGO"!

...NOW WHERE'D I PUT MY STUPID CAR KEYS...
...MUMBLE... ...GRIPE...
BUDDY! BUDDY BRADLEY!
SI, WE'RE OPEN

—WHUH? WHOOZAT?
HEY, HOWYA DOIN'?
IT'S ME, TOM! DON'T YOU REMEMBER ME?
BULL

...I... UH...
TOMMY KAUFMAN! WE WERE BEST FRIENDS IN HIGH SCHOOL, REMEMBER?
? ? ?

—OH MY GOD! I DON'T BELIEVE IT!
AND THIS IS MY SON, AVERY!
—AVERY, I KNEW THIS MAN WHEN WE WERE YOUR AGE!
HUH!

WELL, GEE WHIZ, HOWZIT GOIN', MAN? LONG TIME NO SEE!
OH, IT'S GOIN' PRETTY GOOD— AND I HEAR YOU'RE LIVING AT HOME AGAIN!
BALTO

YEAH, IT'S BEEN TWO YEARS ALREADY... ME AN' OL' "JAY THE JUNKIE" STARTED A BUSINESS TOGETHER, TOO, IF YOU CAN IMAGINE THAT...
...SO I HEAR... IN MY PROFESSION YOU HEAR A LOT OF THINGS...

IZZAT SO? AND WHAT LINE OF WORK ARE YOU IN? ARE YOU A DETECTIVE OR SOMETHING?
EXACTLY! WELL, I'M STILL IN UNIFORM, BUT I SHOULD BE GETTING MY PROMOTION ANY DAY NOW...

REALLY? YOU'RE A COP? NO SH— I MEAN, NO KIDDING!
YUP. WHAT CAN I SAY? IT'S A LIVING...
AND HE DOESN'T LIKE TO BE CALLED A COP!

HEH-HEH...
SAY, YOU SHOULD COME OVER TO MEET THE MISSUS ONE OF THESE DAYS...
YOU'RE MARRIED TOO, AREN'T YA?
ERR... NO... I, UH...

OH... GUESS I HEARD WRONG THEN...
BUT YOU SHOULD COME OVER FOR DINNER, ANYWAY! I'LL GIVE YOU A CALL...
S-SURE! YOU DO THAT... LATER!
LATER!
SO HE'S A COP, HUH? WHY AM I NOT SURPRISED...
HOPE HE CAN'T TELL I'M ABOUT TO DRIVE DRUNK...

WEEKS LATER...
WHERE'S MOM?
SHE'S OUT 'N' ABOUT WITH ONE OF HER FRIENDS...
SHE SHOULD BE GONE ALL DAY...

OH... GOOD!
SO, TELL ME HOW YOUR PSYCHO SESSION WENT YESTER-DAY...
AAH, NOTHING TO TELL, REALLY...
I WANT TO QUIT GOING TO HIM...
PLOP!

YOU DO? HOW COME?
BECAUSE I'M NOT GETTING ANYTHING OUT OF IT!
I JUST LIE THERE WEEK AFTER WEEK RECOUNTING THE SORDID EVENTS OF MY LIFE AND ALL HE DOES IS JOT DOWN NOTES AND MUTTER: "UM-HMM, GO ON" OR "CONTINUE"...
IT'S SO ANNOYING!
X WORD
SPORTS

YES, BUT THESE THINGS TAKE TIME, DON'T THEY?
IT'S BEEN THREE WEEKS ALREADY! AND HE'S YET TO UTTER AN OPINION ABOUT ANYTHING!

I THOUGHT THIS GUY WOULD BE A REAL KNOW-IT-ALL, AUTHORITARIAN TYPE, MAKING FREUDIAN OBSERVATIONS ABOUT EVERYTHING I SAID...
BUT INSTEAD HE'S JUST A BIG BORE!
DID YOU TELL HIM ABOUT YOUR PAST SUICIDE ATTEMPTS?
X WORD

OF COURSE! WITH ALL THE GORY DETAILS!
AND EVEN THAT DIDN'T GET A RISE OUT OF HIM!
I WAS SO INSULTED!
HMMM... IT SOUNDS LIKE YOU EXPECT HIM TO INDULGE AND ENTERTAIN YOU...

WELL, SURE! WHY NOT? I OUGHT TO BE GETTING SOME-THING OUT OF IT, WITH WHAT HE CHARGES!
SOME-TIMES I WONDER IF HE'S EVEN LISTENING TO ME...
=SIGH= ...OH WELL...
SO NOW WHAT?

WELL, A FRIEND FROM WORK SUGGESTED I USE HER THERAPIST, SO I'M THINKING OF MAYBE TRYING HER ON FOR SIZE...
PLUS I'M TOLD SHE'LL PUT YOU ON ANTI-DEPRESSANTS, LIKE, RIGHT AWAY...
OH YEAH? AND IS THAT WHAT YOU WANT?

WELL, YEAH! ISN'T THAT WHAT YOU WANTED, TOO? SO'S I'LL BE MORE UNDER CONTROL, AND EASIER TO DEAL WITH?
WELL SURE, BUT...

BUT WHAT?
WELL, FOR ONE THING, YOU SEEM PERFECTLY UNDER CONTROL RIGHT NOW...
WHY IS THAT, I WONDER?

OH, I'M JUST EXPERIENCING ONE OF MY MORE LUCID PERIODS... ENJOY IT WHILE IT LASTS, SONNY JIM...
OH, I AM, BELIEVE YOU ME...

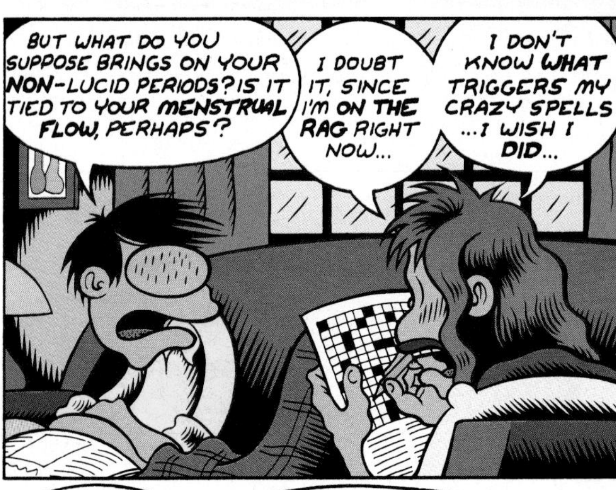
BUT WHAT DO YOU SUPPOSE BRINGS ON YOUR NON-LUCID PERIODS? IS IT TIED TO YOUR MENSTRUAL FLOW, PERHAPS?
I DOUBT IT, SINCE I'M ON THE RAG RIGHT NOW...
I DON'T KNOW WHAT TRIGGERS MY CRAZY SPELLS ...I WISH I DID...

ALL I KNOW IS THAT EVERY NOW AND THEN THE LEAST LITTLE THING CAN SET ME OFF—LIKE THE COLOR OF YOUR SHIRT, FOR EXAMPLE...
IT'S LIKE EVERYTHING IS ALL WRONG, AND THERE'S NOTHING I CAN DO ABOUT IT 'CEPT GO NUTS...
SO YOU—

THAT'S WHEN I START SCREAMING AND THROWING THINGS, 'CUZ I FEEL SO POWERLESS...
THEN I BECOME OVERWHELMED WITH A FEELING OF USELESSNESS AND DISPAIR, WHICH IS WHY I THEN CRAWL INTO BED AND STAY THERE FOR DAYS...
I SEE. SO THERE IS A PATTERN...
I GUESS... MAYBE I'LL START KEEPING A CHART... I'LL CALL IT MY "LOONIE GRAPH"... TEE-HEE!
HA-HA.

I'LL TELL YOU WHAT'S TRULY AMAZING IS HOW WE CAN OCCASIONALLY SIT HERE AND TALK RATIONALLY ABOUT YOUR OWN IRRATIONAL BEHAVIOR...
IT IS UNCANNY, ISN'T IT?

MAYBE YOU HAVE A SPLIT-PERSONALITY —WHAT DO YOU THINK ABOUT THAT?
NAH, 'CUZ I STILL FEEL THE CRAZY PART OF ME ALL THE TIME. IT'S JUST TAKING A BREAK RIGHT NOW...

GOOD, 'CUZ THAT MEANS WE CAN ALL TAKE A BREAK...
AND GIMME S'MORE OF THIS BLANKET —YOU'RE HOGGING IT ALL...
TUG!
WHAT?!? UH-OH, THAT DID IT!
YOU JUST TRIGGERED MY CRAZY BUTTON!
WHA?!? I DID?!?
HA-HA! JUST KIDDING!
SCARED YA, DIDN'T I?

ONE WEEK LATER...

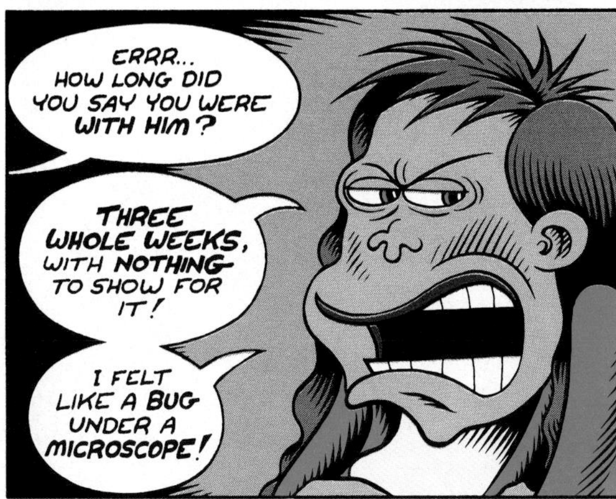

THE NEXT DAY...

...SO ARE YOU READY TO GO OR **WHAT?**

I'M WAITING FOR MY **REPLACEMENT**... JUST BE PATIENT...

—HI, LISA. SORRY I'M **LATE.**

HI, ELIZABETH! I LIKE YOUR **HAIR!**

?

THANKS.

SO, HOW DID YOUR **SESSION** GO?

THE "SESSION"? OH, YOU MEAN WITH YOUR **THERAPIST!** IT WENT **GREAT!** =BURP!=

SHE'S **SUPER NICE**... =BELCH!=

YEAH, SHE'S REALLY **SUPPORTIVE**...

OH, SO **YOU'RE** THE ONE WHO RECOMMENDED LISA'S **NEW SHRINK,** HUH?

SO, YOU THINK YOUR BRAIN MEDICINE IS GIVING YOU GAS, HUH? I WAS WONDERING ABOUT THAT MYSELF...
(OH GHOD, IT'S TERRIBLE! I WISH SOMEONE HAD WARNED ME)...
SALE
50% OFF!!
30%
BAP!
FRAP!
WASTE
EDDIE BAUER
FLURGE
POOT!

OH WELL, AT LEAST THEY'RE NOT THE REAL SMELLY KIND...
OH, LISA!
FOOP!
FART!

?!? WHAT'S UP, LIZ?
DID YOU EVER SUGGEST TO YOUR FRIEND HERE ABOUT THE... YOU KNOW...

ABOUT THE..?!... OH, YOU MEAN THE JOINT SESSION!
?!? THE WHAT?

OOPS!
?
(NO, I HAVEN'T YET... I'LL TALK TO YOU ABOUT IT LATER)...
(GOOD LUCK... YOU'LL PROBABLY NEED IT!)

...WHAT'S ALL THIS ABOUT A "JOINT SESSION"? DOES THAT MEAN WHAT I THINK IT DOES?
(SHH! NOT SO LOUD!)
(AND THERE'S NO REASON TO BE ALARMED, 'CUZ IT'S GOT NOTHING TO DO WITH YOU)...

...LIZ JUST THINKS IT WOULD BE A GOOD IDEA IF YOU SAT IN ON ONE OF MY SESSIONS, IS ALL...
YEAH, RIGHT. I CAN TELL BY THE WAY SHE LOOKS AT ME THAT SHE THINKS I'M YOUR BIGGEST "MENTAL PROBLEM."
PRESUMPTUOUS LITTLE BITCH! I HATE HER ALREADY!

OH YEAH, RIGHT. I SAW YOU CHECKING OUT HER BUTT... I BET YOU WANT TO FUCK HER...
THAT'S RIGHT. I WANT TO FUCK HER, AND THEN I WANT TO SLIT HER THROAT...

—OMIGOSH, WHAT A HORRIBLE THING TO SAY... SORRY ABOUT THAT...
AH-HA-HA-HA-HA! NO NEED TO APOLOGIZE —I LIKE IT WHEN YOU'RE HONEST!
SLAP!

...EWWWW... EVERY TIME I LAUGH ANOTHER FART SLIPS OUT...
FRIPP!

WEEKS LATER...
...LISA? IS THAT YOU OVER THERE?
YES, AND DON'T TURN THE LIGHT ON...

BUT, I CAN BARELY—
DON'T TURN IT ON!
...I LIKE IT THIS WAY...

OHHH-KAY...
ANYHOW, I JUST GOT OFF THE PHONE WITH MY OLD CLASSMATE TOM...
WHO?

REMEMBER, I TOLD YOU I BUMPED INTO HIM A FEW WEEKS BACK?
WELL, HE JUST INVITED US OVER FOR DINNER, AND—
I'M NOT GOING.

?!? BUT, I JUST TOLD HIM WE WOULD, AND—
FINE, YOU GO! I'LL BE PERFECTLY FINE HERE BY MYSELF...

ARE YOU SURE? I MEAN, IT'S BEEN MONTHS SINCE WE'VE BEEN INVITED TO ANYTHING...
LOOK, IF YOU WANNA GO THEN GO! I'M NOT TRYING TO STOP YOU...
...I'M JUST NOT IN THE MOOD FOR THAT TYPE OF SCENE...

"SCENE"? SINCE WHEN DOES GOING TO SOMEONE'S HOUSE FOR DINNER CONSTITUTE A "SCENE"?
YOU'D THINK I WAS TRYING TO DRAG YOU TO A "RAVE" OR SOME-THING...
=SIGH=

...BUDDY, I'M JUST NOT IN THE MOOD, OKAY? SO PLEASE LEAVE ME ALONE, OKAY?
GO SEE YOUR FRIEND, HAVE A GOOD TIME, AND DON'T WORRY ABOUT ME, 'CUZ I'LL BE FINE...
OKAY, OKAY...

NOW IF YOU DON'T MIND, I'D LIKE TO...
I'M ON MY WAY...JUST AS SOON AS I CHANGE MY SOCKS...

BUMP!
OW! JEEZIZ...
...I CAN'T SEE A THING...

CLICK!
GAAH!
TURN OFF THAT LIGHT!

HOLD ON... I JUST HAVE TO FIND A CLEAN PAIR OF SOCKS...
OH GOD... PLEASE HURRY UP...
FLING!
TOSS!

...WHIMPER...
?

LISA, ARE YOU SURE YOU'RE OKAY? 'CUZ YOU SURE DON'T LOOK OKAY...
I'M JUST DEPRESSED, IS ALL...
I'LL GET OVER IT...
EVENTUALLY...

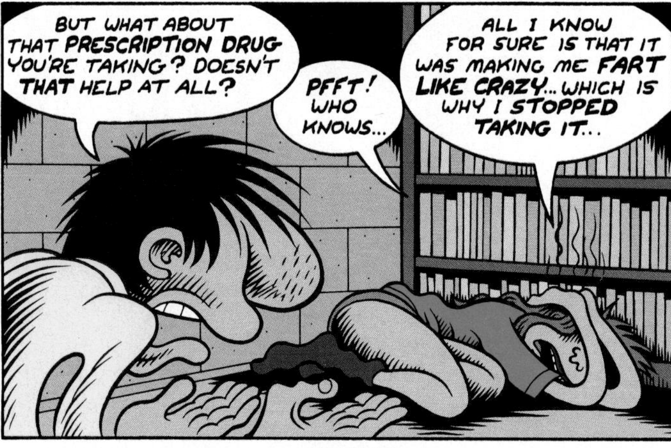
BUT WHAT ABOUT THAT PRESCRIPTION DRUG YOU'RE TAKING? DOESN'T THAT HELP AT ALL?
PFFT! WHO KNOWS...
ALL I KNOW FOR SURE IS THAT IT WAS MAKING ME FART LIKE CRAZY... WHICH IS WHY I STOPPED TAKING IT...

YOU WHAT?!
BUT, W—
DON'T LECTURE ME, OKAY?
IF YOU THINK THAT STUFF IS SO GREAT THEN YOU TAKE IT! THEN AT LEAST WE COULD COMPARE NOTES!

...DOES YOUR THERAPIST KNOW ABOUT THIS?
NO, AND DON'T YOU GO SQUEALING ON ME, EITHER...

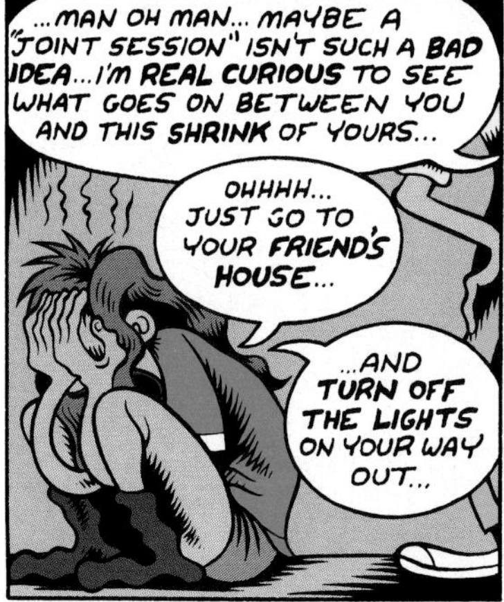
...MAN OH MAN... MAYBE A "JOINT SESSION" ISN'T SUCH A BAD IDEA... I'M REAL CURIOUS TO SEE WHAT GOES ON BETWEEN YOU AND THIS SHRINK OF YOURS...
OHHHH... JUST GO TO YOUR FRIEND'S HOUSE...
...AND TURN OFF THE LIGHTS ON YOUR WAY OUT...

FINE, I'M GOING...
AND WHEN I GET BACK MAYBE I'LL WRITE A "SCENE REPORT" FOR YA...
THAT'S A JOKE, GET IT?
CLICK

SLAM!
...HA-HA. VERY FUNNY.

AND SO...
DINNER SHOULD BE READY ANY MINUTE, FELLOWS...
SORRY IT'S TAKING SO LONG...
WHAT MUSIC IS THIS WE'RE LISTENING TO, TOM?
WHY, DO YOU LIKE IT?
...WELCOME TO THE HOME OF THE BLUES...
BLEEP! BLOOP! BZZZT!

...BUT BY THE TIME I GOT OUT OF COLLEGE I'D COMPLETELY GIVEN UP ON THIS WHOLE NOTION OF "HIPNESS," AND FINALLY ACCEPTED MYSELF AS THE HOPELESS NERD THAT I AM...
...PRETTY PATHETIC, HUH?
QUITE THE CONTRARY — IT'S ADMIRABLE!
OKAY, DINNER'S READY!
MMMM... THAT SPAGHETTI SMELLS GOOD...
UM-HMM!
OFF WITH THE T.V., YOUNG MAN! YOU KNOW THE RULES!
OKAY, OKAY...
CLICK!
...MILK OR JUICE, AVERY?
MILK — NO, JUICE!
CHEESE ON YOUR NOODLES OR NO?
YES CHEESE!
SO, FLORA, WHAT'S IT LIKE TO BE MARRIED TO KOJAK OVAH HEAH?
"KOJAK" —HA! "BARNEY MILLER" IS MORE LIKE IT...
HA!
HE'S YET TO HAVE ANYONE EVEN PULL A GUN ON HIM—KNOCK ON WOOD...
PASS THE BUTTER!
HEY, HOW DO WE ASK?
PLEASE!
THAT'S MORE LIKE IT...
JUST BECAUSE WE HAVE A GUEST DOESN'T MEAN WE CAN BACK-SLIDE ON OUR MANNERS...
YES, SIR...
HERE YA GO, AVERY.
THANK YOU.
THIS KID'S A SAINT COMPARED TO MY SISTER'S BRATS!
...BUT YEAH, MY JOB IS NOTHING LIKE WHAT YOU SEE ON T.V...
IN FACT, SOMETIMES IT SEEMS LIKE THE ENTIRE POLICE FORCE IS JUST A BUNCH OF BABYSITTERS, WHOSE JOB IS TO MAKE SURE THE LOWER CLASSES BEHAVE THEMSELVES...
OH BOY, HERE WE GO...
ALL RIGHT, I DON'T MEAN ALL POOR PEOPLE PER SE, BUT IT'S AMAZING HOW MANY PEOPLE REACH ADULTHOOD WITHOUT EVER LEARNING HOW TO LIVE BY SOCIETY'S RULES, AND IT SEEMS LIKE WE SPEND 95% OF OUR TIME CHASING AFTER THEM AND CLEANING UP THEIR MESSES...
AND EVERY NOW AND THEN YOU PUT THE REAL INCORRIGIBLE ONES IN JAIL, JUST LIKE YOU GIVE A KID A "TIME OUT" WHEN HE MISBEHAVES...
YEESH.
OF COURSE, THESE ARE MURDERERS AND RAPISTS WE'RE TALKING ABOUT, DEAR...
I KNOW IT SOUNDS LIKE A STRETCH, BUT THE ANALOGY RINGS TRUER TO ME ALL THE TIME...
...ESPECIALLY AS I WATCH MY OWN SON GROW UP...
I CAN SEE HOW YOUR JOB COULD MAKE YOU CYNICAL TOWARDS ALL HUMANITY...
...IF I WERE YOU I'D BE FILLED WITH CONTEMPT...

YEAH, IT GETS TO ME, BUT I TRY TO KEEP THINGS IN PERSPECTIVE...
...THAT'S PARTLY WHY I'M GLAD I'M ATTENDING CHURCH AGAIN...
HUH?! DID YOU SAY "CHURCH"?
B-BUT, YOU AND I USED TO ALWAYS MAKE FUN OF—
I KNOW, I KNOW. DON'T REMIND ME...
DON'T BLAME ME. IT WAS ALL TOM'S IDEA...
...I AGREED TO START ATTENDING FOR AVERY'S SAKE, BUT NOW TOM'S REALLY GOTTEN INTO IT...
OH REALLY?
UM-HMM...HE GETS INTO THESE HEATED DISCUSSIONS WITH THE PRIESTS OVER THEIR SERMONS AND WHATNOT, WHILE I COULDN'T CARE LESS...
...I MOSTLY JUST SIT THERE AND CHECK OUT WHAT EVERYONE ELSE IS WEARING...
THAT'S WHAT I'D BE DOING!
AND THAT'S WHAT I USED TO DO...
BUT ONCE I STARTED TO PAY ATTENTION TO WHAT THE PRIESTS WERE SAYING I FOUND MYSELF GETTING ALL WORKED UP...
SO I DECIDED TO GIVE THEM MY INPUT, RATHER THAN JUST BE A PASSIVE SPECTATOR...
HO-HUM...
—WHAT'S THE MATTER, AVERY?
THIS CONVERSATION IS BORING!
HA-HA!
HEY AVERY, WHY DON'T YOU SHOW BUDDY WHAT YOU MADE ON YOUR COMPUTER?
OKAY!
LEAP!
?!? WHAT'S HE GONNA SHOW ME?
YOU'LL SEE...
ZIP!
...HERE YA GO!
WOW... WHAT IS THIS?
IT'S AN ARCHITECTURAL LAYOUT FOR AN ACTUAL CASTLE, ALL DONE ON HIS COMPUTER!
HE GOT THE IDEA FROM A BOOK, BUT THE DESIGN IS ALL HIS OWN...
ISN'T IT AMAZING?
I'LL SAY... I'M FLABBERGASTED!
I DON'T KNOW THE FIRST THING ABOUT COMPUTERS...
I FEEL SO... ALIENATED!

LATER THAT NIGHT...
...ZZZZZ...
GOOD, SHE'S SOUND ASLEEP...

?!?
I JUST STEPPED INTO SOMETHING WET AND GROSS!
WHAT IS THIS? PUKE!
SPLORSH!

EWWWW... IT LOOKS LIKE A PLATE OF TURNED-OVER SPAGHETTI-O'S!
HOW DISGUSTING!

...IT'S ALL OVER THE WALLS, TOO! IT'S EVERYWHERE!
WHAT THE HELL HAPPENED!

LISA, WAKE UP! WHAT'S GOING ON AROUND HERE?!
...ZZZZK! —HUH?!? WHAT ARE YOU TALKING ABOUT?
SHAKE! SHAKE!

THIS ROOM! THERE'S FOOD SPLATTERED ALL OVER THE PLACE!
HOW DID IT GET THIS WAY?
OH JEEZ, I DON'T KNOW... HOW SHOULD I KNOW?
I JUST WANNA GO TO SLEEP...

?!? WHADAYA MEAN, YOU DON'T KNOW?
YOU'VE EVEN GOT SPAGHETTI-O'S ALL OVER YOUR T-SHIRT!
...SO? WHAT'S YOUR POINT?

...YA KNOW, I REALLY WISH YOU'D STOP WORRYING ABOUT EVERY LITTLE THING AND LET ME GET SOME SLEEP!!!

...CHRIST... YOU'RE ALWAYS BLAMING ME FOR EVERYTHING...
...I WISH FOR ONCE YOU'D JUST LEAVE ME ALONE...
FLOP!
?!?

...ZZZZ...
...MUTTER... GRIPE...

...IF THERE IS A GOD, HE MUST BE PUNISHING ME FOR SOMETHING...

ONE WEEK LATER...

...NOW, PART OF THE PURPOSE OF A JOINT SESSION IS SO THAT I CAN WITNESS **FIRST HAND** HOW THE TWO OF YOU **INTERACT**, AND THEN BETTER UNDERSTAND THE **DYNAMICS OF YOUR RELATIONSHIP**...

=GRUNT=

...IT WAS **QUITE THE OPPOSITE,** I'M SORRY TO SAY...
...GUESS I WAS TOO "**EMOTIONALLY DETACHED**" TO ACKNOWLEDGE THE **STUPIDITY** OF THE WHOLE SITUATION...
YES, WELL, WE'RE NOT HERE TO ARGUE OVER EVENTS OF THE **PAST**...

...WHAT WE SHOULD BE **MORE** CONCERNED WITH IS THE **HERE AND NOW,** AND RIGHT NOW LISA STRIKES ME AS A YOUNG WOMAN WHO'S **EVOLVING AND GROWING** AS A PERSON...
AND LIKE A BUTTERFLY IN ITS COCOON SHE NEEDS TO **BREAK FREE** IN ORDER TO **SURVIVE** AND **THRIVE**...
OH BROTHER...

...ONLY HER CURRENT LIVING SITUATION IS **PREVENTING** HER FROM DOING SO...
...WOULD YOU **AGREE** WITH THAT ASSESSMENT, BUDDY?
WHAT, THAT LISA'S LIKE A **BUTTERFLY?** NO, I DON'T AGREE WITH THAT **AT ALL**...

YOU **DON'T**. WELL THEN, HOW WOULD **YOU** DESCRIBE HER?
TEE-HEE!
WELL, TO ME SHE SEEMS MORE LIKE A **MOLE**... A MOLE THAT'S TRYING TO DIG ITSELF **DEEPER** AND **DEEPER** INTO THE **EARTH**...

HMMMM... **INTERESTING**...
—HMM? **WHAT?** I DON'T—
...WHAT DO YOU MAKE OF **BUDDY'S ANALOGY,** LISA?

ABOUT YOUR BEING LIKE A **MOLE**... WOULD YOU SAY THAT'S **ACCURATE?**
OH, GEE, I DUNNO... I THOUGHT IT WAS **PRETTY FUNNY,** THOUGH...

—W-**WHAT?** DID I SAY SOMETHING **WRONG?**

...SIGH... LISA, I THINK IT'S IMPORTANT FOR YOU TO REMEMBER THAT YOU'RE **NOT AT HOME** RIGHT NOW...
THIS IS A **NEUTRAL ENVIRONMENT,** AND AS SUCH YOU SHOULD FEEL AS FREE TO EXPRESS YOURSELF AS YOU DO IN OUR **PRIVATE SESSIONS**...
HEY! WHAT'S **THAT** SUPPOSED TO MEAN?

—I BEG YOUR **PARDON?** I WAS ONLY—
"DON'T WORRY, LISA, HE WON'T **SLUG YA** AS LONG AS **I'M** AROUND."
THAT'S WHAT IT SOUNDED LIKE TO **ME!**

OH PUH-LEASE! IF YOU COULD JUST REFRAIN FROM JUMPING TO CONCLUSIONS, I—
OH, SO NOW I'M "JUMPING TO CONCLUSIONS," AM I?
I THOUGHT THE WHOLE IDEA WAS FOR US TO "EXPRESS OURSELVES FREELY"!
BUT APPARENTLY THERE'S A "RIGHT" AND "WRONG" ANSWER FOR EVERYTHING WITH YOU—
MAY I INTERJECT HERE FOR A MOMENT?
...THE REASON I'M TRYING TO DRAW LISA OUT IS BECAUSE HER COMMENTS— IN FACT HER ENTIRE DEMEANOR— ARE DRASTICALLY DIFFERENT TODAY THAN FROM OUR PREVIOUS VISITS...
THAT'S BECAUSE SHE WAS ONLY TELLING YOU WHAT YOU WANTED TO HEAR, AND SHE KNOWS I'LL CALL HER ON IT ONCE SHE TRIED TO FEED YOU HER BULLSHIT!
...AND YOU'RE SO CAUGHT UP IN YOUR OWN AGENDA THAT YOU CAN'T EVEN SEE WHEN YOU'RE BEING HAD!
I BEG YOUR PARDON!
...I HAPPEN TO BE A HIGHLY RESPECTED PROFESSIONAL WITH A LONG, SUCCESSFUL TRACK RECORD!
AND I INVITE YOU TO CONTACT ANY OF MY REFERENCES IF YOU DOUBT MY VERACITY!
YEAH, YEAH, YEAH...
...AND TALK ABOUT AGENDAS! IT SOUNDS TO ME LIKE YOU'VE BEEN LISTENING TO TOO MUCH RIGHT-WING RADIO!
ARRRGH....
=AHEM=... NOW, LET'S SEE IF WE CAN AT LEAST ACCOMPLISH SOMETHING CONSTRUCTIVE WITH WHAT TIME WE HAVE LEFT WITH THIS VISIT...
...AND LISA, I'D STILL LIKE TO GET SOME FEEDBACK FROM YOU REGARDING BUDDY'S EARLIER COMMENTS...
YES, LISA, PLEASE SPEAK FREELY...
...I'LL MAKE SURE THAT YOUR THERAPIST DOESN'T SLUG YA IF YOU GIVE THE WRONG ANSWER...
TEE-HEE! GIGGLE!

AND SO...
PROFESSIONAL BUILDING
WELL, THAT WAS FUN, WASN'T IT?
NO COMMENT.

BIG FUN
MOTHER'S WORRY

VAROOOMM...
BUDDA BUDDA BUDDA...

...I GOTTA ADMIT, THOUGH, THAT THAT THERAPIST OF MINE SURE IS AN ASSHOLE...
—WHAT?!?
FORD.

B-BUT, I THOUGHT YOU WORSHIPPED THE GROUND SHE WALKED ON!
AAH, I GUESS I JUST LIKED THE WAY SHE INDULGED ME AND MADE UP EXCUSES FOR MY BEHAVIOR...

...BUT YOU SURE HIT THE NAIL ON THE HEAD WHEN YOU ACCUSED HER OF HAVING AN AGENDA...
YA THINK SO? =WHEW!= THANKS...
I WAS WORRIED THAT I MAY HAVE BEEN A BIT OUT OF LINE WITH THAT REMARK...

OF COURSE, YOU HAVE AN "AGENDA," TOO...
EVERYBODY'S GOT AN AGENDA, EXCEPT FOR ME...
WHICH I GUESS IS WHY I'M SO FUCKED UP...
I, UHH... HMMM...

...BUDDY?
YES?

...WHAT WOULD YOU DO IF I TOLD YOU I WAS HAVING AN AFFAIR WITH MY FRIEND ELIZABETH?

...WHAT WOULD I DO, YOU ASK? BOY, THAT'S A GOOD ONE...
WELL?

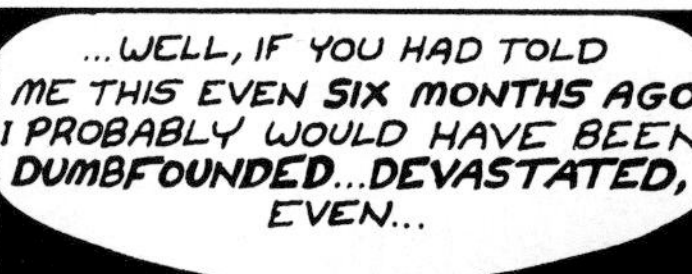
...WELL, IF YOU HAD TOLD ME THIS EVEN SIX MONTHS AGO I PROBABLY WOULD HAVE BEEN DUMBFOUNDED...DEVASTATED, EVEN...

...BUT AT THIS POINT I'M SO COMPLETELY BURNED-OUT BY YOUR SHENANIGANS THAT I PROBABLY WOULDN'T FEEL ANYTHING...
IN FACT, I'D PROBABLY FEEL RELIEVED...
RELIEVED? REALLY? WHY?

WHY? BECAUSE THAT WOULD SPELL THE END FOR THE TWO OF US, WOULDN'T IT?
...AND THEN I'D NO LONGER FEEL RESPONSIBLE FOR YOUR EMOTIONAL WELL-BEING...
YOU'D BE SOMEBODY ELSE'S PROBLEM BY THEN...
HMMM...

...WHY, ARE YOU HAVING AN AFFAIR WITH HER?
NAH... ARE YOU KIDDING? I COULDN'T GET INTO THAT LEZBO STUFF...

...I JUST SAID THAT IN ORDER TO GAUGE HOW SICK OF ME YOU MUST BE BY NOW...
OH...

...WELP, JUDGING FROM MY RESPONSE, I GUESS THERE'S NO POINT IN DENYING THAT I'M PRETTY FUCKING SICK OF YOU AND YOUR "MENTAL PROBLEMS."

...SO I GOTTA ADMIT THAT THAT WAS A PRETTY EFFECTIVE "GAUGE" YOU CAME UP WITH...
THANKS. I THOUGHT IT WOULD DO THE TRICK...

...BOO-HOO-HOO -HOO-HOO...
OH BROTHER, HERE WE GO...

GREAT GOD IN HEAVEN! WHEN WILL THIS VICIOUS CIRCLE BE BROKEN?!?

BUDDY and LISA in

IT HAD TO HAPPEN

DRAT...
...HAS ANYONE SEEN MY **CAR KEYS**?
NOPE.
DID YOU CHECK THE POCKETS OF THE CLOTHES YOU WORE **YESTERDAY?**
VOICE
WORLD'S GREATEST MOM

NO, BECAUSE I WEAR THE **SAME CLOTHES EVERY DAY**...
DAMN, WHERE DID I **PUT THEM?** I'M LATE FOR WORK ALREADY...
BY THE WAY, BUDDY, I —

—AH-HAH! THERE THEY ARE!
...NICE OF YOU TO TELL ME THEY WERE **RIGHT UNDER YOUR NOSE,** LISA...
—HUH?
GRAB!
VOICE
SPECIAL ALL GAY ISSUE!

...I JUST WANTED TO TELL YOU BEFORE YOU HEAD OUT THAT I WON'T BE HOME 'TIL **LATE** TONIGHT BECAUSE I'M GOING OUT ON A **DATE**...
OKAY, FINE. SEE YOU **LATER**...

—YOU WHAT?!?

...DID YOU SAY A "DATE"?
B-BUT, WHO... WHAT... HOW...
IT'S NO ONE YOU KNOW, JUST A FRIEND OF A FRIEND FROM WORK...

AND IT'S NOTHING SERIOUS, SO DON'T SEND OUT THE WEDDING INVITATIONS JUST YET...
I JUST NEED A REASON TO GET OUT OF THE HOUSE, IS ALL...
HUH. WELL, I'LL BE...
ITCH ITCH!

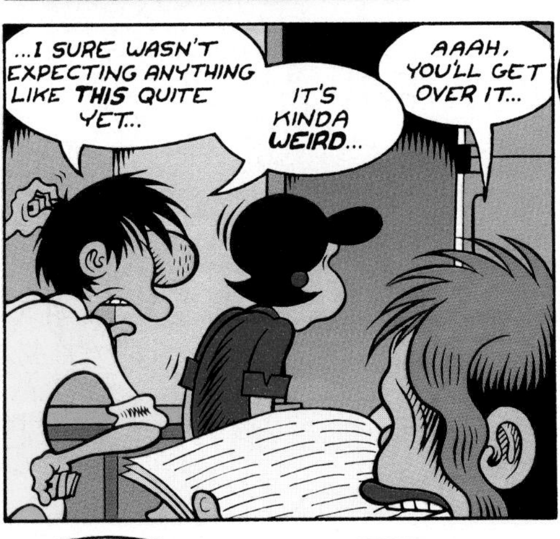
...I SURE WASN'T EXPECTING ANYTHING LIKE THIS QUITE YET...
IT'S KINDA WEIRD...
AAAH, YOU'LL GET OVER IT...

HMM? OH, I'M SURE I WILL...
BUT I CAN'T HELP BUT NOTICE THAT YOU DON'T SEEM THE LEAST BIT FAZED BY THIS BIT OF NEWS, LISA...
THAT'S BECAUSE I ALREADY TOLD HER...
THAT'S RIGHT. IT'S OLD NEWS TO ME, JACK.
VOICE

IS THAT SO? AND WHY WAS I KEPT IN THE DARK FOR SO LONG?
SINCE WHEN CAN ANYONE INFORM YOU OF ANYTHING? YOU'RE ALWAYS SO BUSY AND DISTRACTED...
AND LIKE YOUR MA SAID: IT'S NO BIG DEAL...
VOIC

OKAY, SO IT'S NO BIG DEAL...
—OH MAN, LOOK AT THE TIME! I GOTTA RUN...
YOU WANT ME TO DRIVE YOU TO WORK, LISA?
NAH...

...I'M GETTING A RIDE FROM MY FRIEND, ELIZABETH.
FROM WHO?

...OH... ...HER...

WELP, GIVE HER MY REGARDS...
SO LONG...
'BYE.

SLAM!

...Y'KNOW, LISA, I GOTTA CONFESS THAT I'M **REALLY NERVOUS** ABOUT THIS "DATE" I'M GOING ON...
REALLY? **WHY?**

I DUNNO... I JUST...
'CUZ YOU SAID IT'S JUST A **CASUAL THING,** RIGHT? IN FACT, ISN'T IT A "**DOUBLE DATE**"?
VOICE

'CUZ DIDN'T YOU SAY YOUR FRIEND **GLORIA** AND **HER HUSBAND** WERE GOING ALONG, TOO? SO YOU WON'T EVEN BE **ALONE** WITH THE GUY!
I KNOW, BUT... **GOD,** IT'S SO **EMBARRASSING**! IT'S BEEN **DECADES** SINCE I'VE BEEN IN A SITUATION LIKE THIS, WHERE I'LL BE **SIZING SOMEBODY UP** AS A POTENTIAL **MATE**...

...AND HE'LL BE "**SIZING ME UP**" AS WELL! **OH MY GOD**...
RELAX, "MOM"! YOU'RE **THINKING ABOUT IT** TOO MUCH...

JUST GO OUT AND **HAVE FUN**! AND IF IT **DOES** LEAD TO SOMETHING THEN JUST THINK OF IT AS A **BONUS**!
NOTHING VENTURED, NOTHING GAINED, RIGHT?
OH, I SUPPOSE...

MY PHILOSOPHY HAS ALWAYS BEEN THAT IT'S BETTER TO **DIVE RIGHT INTO THE UNKNOWN**—EVEN IF IT LEADS TO **DISASTER**— THAN TO STICK WITH THE **BORING** AND **FAMILIAR**...
HMMM... **INTERESTING**...
I DIDN'T KNOW YOU WERE THE **PHILOSOPHICAL TYPE,** LISA...

WELL, THAT'S MY **ONLY** PHILOSOPHY, BUT YA GOTTA ADMIT IT'S A **GOOD ONE**!
DING! DONG!
— WHO COULD **THAT** BE?

OH, THAT SHOULD BE MY **RIDE**...
'BYE, "MOM", AND **GOOD LUCK**!
THANKS.

...READY?
READY AS I'LL EVER BE...

LATER THAT DAY, AT "B+J'S COLLECTOR'S EMPORIUM"...
...SO C'MON DOWN, PLACE YOUR **BID**, AND DRIVE AWAY WITH THE **CAR**, **BOAT** OR **R.V.** OF YOUR **DREAMS**...
LISTEN TO THIS— IT'S ANOTHER AUCTION FOR ALL THE **LOOT** THE **COPS CONFISCATE** ON THEIR **DRUG BUSTS**...
WHAT A **RACKET!**
IT'S THE **SPOILS OF WAR** IS WHAT IT IS...
KNOCK! KNOCK!
Radio Haiku
WHAM
JAMES LAST
NANCY & LEE LIVE!
RECORD SWAP
SUB POP
PIECES OF Felix

EXCUSE ME, I—
WE'RE **CLOSED**, PAL.

BUT, I JUST—
DON'T YOU SEE THE **SIGN** ON THE **DOOR**? IT SAYS: "**BACK BY 2PM**"!

ER, **YES**, BUT SINCE IT'S NOW FIVE MINUTES **PAST** TWO, I THOUGHT—
WE'RE EATING OUR LUNCH! NOW GET OUT OF HERE!
WE'LL BE BACK BY:

?!? **GOOD GRIEF!**
...SAY, WHATEVER HAPPENED TO THOSE **EGG**, **PEPPER** AND **POTATO SANDWICHES** LISA USED TO MAKE FOR YOU?
ZIP!

ACTUALLY, MY **MOM** USED TO MAKE THOSE FOR ME, AND LISA WOULD WRAP 'EM IN **TIN FOIL** TO KEEP 'EM **WARM**...
...NOW **NEITHER** OF THEM COULD BE BOTHERED, SO I'M LEFT TO MY **OWN DEVICES**...
WHICH MEANS **PEANUT BUTTER SANDWICHES** FIVE DAYS A WEEK...

ERRRR... **RIGHT**.
=SIGH= TOO BAD FOR **YOU**...
...THOSE SANDWICHES WERE **TASTY**...

CHOMP!
SLURP!

UHHHH... I HATE TO BRING UP WHAT MAY BE A **SORE SUBJECT**, BUT—
—HOW ARE THINGS BETWEEN ME 'N' LISA? **NOT BAD**, TO TELL YOU THE TRUTH...

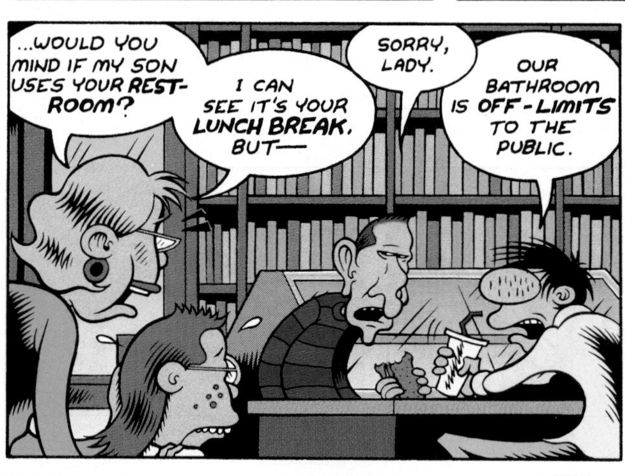

...I GUESS I PREFER THINGS TO BE BORING AND PREDICTABLE THAN TO HAVE TO DEAL WITH THE NEW AND UNPREDICTABLE...

HUH...

"THE PHILOSOPHY OF BUDDY BRADLEY."

...AND NOW BACK TO DOCTOR LAURA...

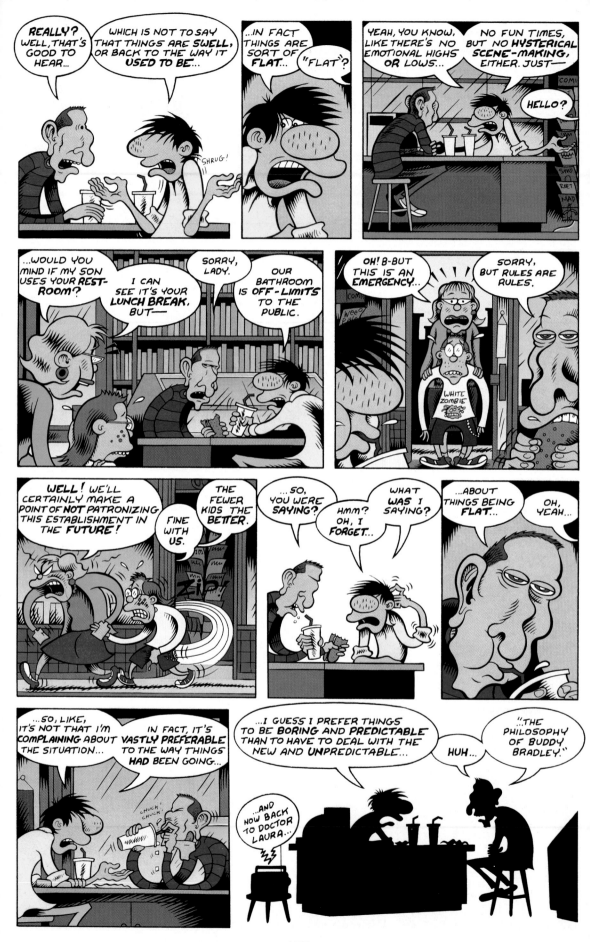

THAT EVENING...
OH MAN, WHAT A DAY...
TRUDGE TRUDGE

BARGE!
HELLO? IS ANYBODY HOME?

HMMM... WHAT'S THIS?
LOOKS LIKE A MESSAGE FROM MOMMY DEAREST...

Buddy + Lisa
Decided to
"Date" into a wee
end thing, so we
be in the Pocono
til late Sund
night.
Plenty of food
in the fridge.
—Mom
Over →

THERE'S MORE ON THE BACK...
..."I'LL BE SHARING A ROOM WITH GLORIA, SO GET YOUR MIND OUT OF THE GUTTER! —M."
FLIP!

...FEH. AS IF I CARE WHETHER SHE'S GETTING BANGED OR NOT...
OH WELL, AT LEAST I'LL HAVE THE HOUSE TO MYSELF UNTIL LISA GETS HOME...
TOSS!

ONE HOUR LATER...
...AHHHH... NOW THIS IS HOW IT SHOULD BE — KING OF MY OWN CASTLE!
...WATCHING WHAT I WANNA WATCH, WHEN I WANNA WATCH IT, ALL FROM THE COMFORT OF MY OWN EASY CHAIR...
...I REALLY SHOULD GET A PLACE OF MY OWN ONE OF THESE DAYS...
CLICK! CLICK! CLICK!
...NEXT ON "SPORTS-CENTER"...
ESPN

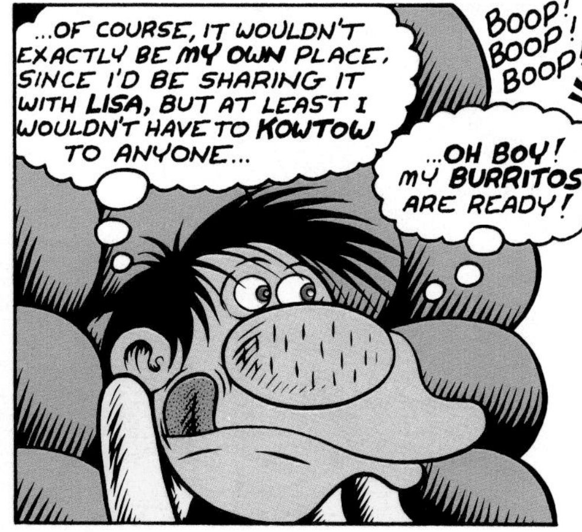
...OF COURSE, IT WOULDN'T EXACTLY BE MY OWN PLACE, SINCE I'D BE SHARING IT WITH LISA, BUT AT LEAST I WOULDN'T HAVE TO KOWTOW TO ANYONE...
BOOP! BOOP! BOOP!
...OH BOY! MY BURRITOS ARE READY!

MORE TIME PASSES...
AHHH... THAT BURRITO WAS GOOD...
...I THINK I'LL INDULGE MYSELF AND HAVE A BEER, THOUGH I PROBABLY SHOULD WAIT UNTIL LISA GETS HOME...
TWO OUT IN THE BOTTOM OF THE ...SIXTH
PAT PAT

AAH, FUCK IT! IT'S FRIDAY NIGHT AND I'M ENTITLED!
LISA SHOULDA BEEN HOME BY NOW ANYWAY...
LEAP!

...AHHHH... THAT HITS THE SPOT!
...I WONDER WHAT'S KEEPING LISA, ANYWAY?
OH WELL, WHO CARES...

YET MORE TIME PASSES...
...ARRGH! FUCKIN' METS GOT THEIR ASSES KICKED AGAIN!
AND WHERE THE FUCK IS LISA? IT'S PAST ELEVEN ALREADY!
CLICK!

...THAT VIDEO STORE SHE WORKS AT IS NEVER OPEN THIS LATE, BUT I'LL TRY CALLING HER THERE ANYWAY, JUST IN CASE...

...OUR HOURS ARE 10 AM TO 10 PM FRIDAY THROUGH SUNDAY, AND—
CLICK!
DAMN, CLOSED. JUST LIKE I FIGURED...
WHERE COULD SHE BE? MY SISTER'S MAYBE?

AND SO...
RING! RING—
BABS? THIS IS BUDDY. IS LISA THERE, BY ANY CHANCE?
HELLO?

NO, SHE ISN'T...
BUT I'M GLAD YOU CALLED, 'CUZ I WANT TO GET YOUR OPINION ABOUT MOM DATING...
ABOUT WHAT?
OH, JEEZ, I DUNNO...

WELL, I FOR ONE AM TOTALLY AGAINST IT! IT'S WAY TOO SOON FOR HER TO BE SEEING OTHER MEN!
SHE'S LEAVING HERSELF WIDE OPEN FOR SOME NO GOOD—
YEAH, WELL, I DON'T WANT TO TALK ABOUT IT RIGHT NOW, SO... GOOD-BYE!
...MOM...
MOM, TYLER'S KEEPING ME UP...

WAIT! DON'T—
YEESH! GET A LIFE, YOU JEALOUS SHREW!
SLAM!

NOW, WHERE THE HELL COULD SHE BE...
...THINK... THINK...
PACE
PACE

...AH-HA! I'LL BET SHE'S WITH THAT HORRID LITTLE FRIEND OF HERS, ELIZABETH!

THAT WOULD EXPLAIN A LOT, CONSIDERING HOW MUCH THAT LITTLE WITCH HATES ME...
SHE PROBABLY WON'T LET LISA CALL ME TO TELL ME WHERE SHE IS!
...NOW WHAT WAS HER NAME AGAIN?
...SOME-THING JEWISH SOUNDING... STARTS WITH AN "M"...
..."MIZEL", MAYBE?..
..AH-HA! "E. MIZELL"...
THAT'S GOTTA BE HER!
...THIS MAY BE A WILD GOOSE CHASE, BUT IT'S WORTH A SHOT...
RING! RING! RIN—
HELLO, THIS IS "GOTH CENTRAL STATION"... =SNICKER=
?!?
UHHH, I-IS ELIZABETH THERE?
HOLD ON, I'LL GO CHECK...
"GOTH"? IS THAT WHAT SHE'S SUPPOSED TO BE, A "GOTH CHICK"?
OH WELL, SHOWS HOW MUCH I KNOW...
...JEEZ...I CAN HEAR HIM ASKING HALF A DOZEN PEOPLE IF THEY KNOW WHERE SHE IS, AND NOT ONE OF 'EM HAS A CLUE...
I GUESS IT'S NOT VERY "GOTH" TO KEEP TRACK OF YOUR ROOM-MATES...
...SORRY, SHE'S NOT HERE SOMEONE SAID THEY WENT INTO THE CITY TO CATCH A SHOW...
"THEY"?
YEAH, HER AND HER FRIEND... I FORGOT HER NAME...
IT WOULDN'T BE LISA, WOULD IT? SHE'S SHORT, WITH RED HAIR...THEY WORK AT THE SAME PLACE...
—OH YEAH, THAT'S THE ONE! "LISA", IS THAT HER NAME? YEAH, THAT'S WHO SHE WENT WITH...
...UHH, DO YOU WANT ME TO LEAVE A MESSAGE?

MANY HOURS LATER...
RING! RING! RING!
GROANNN...
...ZZZZZZK? WHO THE HELL...

...HELLO?
JAY, THIS IS BUDDY...

UGHHH... BUDDY, DO YOU REALIZE WHAT TIME IT IS? IT'S ALMOST FOUR...
THAT'S EXACTLY WHY I'M CALLING! LISA WENT TO THE CITY TONIGHT WITHOUT EVEN TELLING ME, AND I HAVE NO IDEA WHEN SHE'S COMING BACK!

UH-HUH. AND WHY ARE YOU TELLING ME ALL OF THIS?
BECAUSE I'M FREAKING OUT AND I HAVE TO TELL SOMEONE!
?

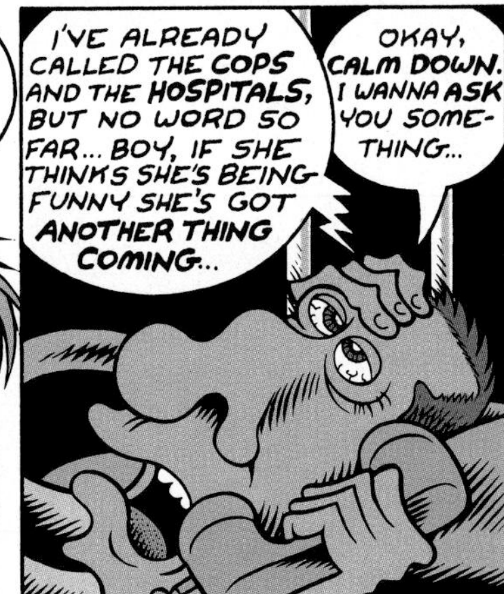
I'VE ALREADY CALLED THE COPS AND THE HOSPITALS, BUT NO WORD SO FAR... BOY, IF SHE THINKS SHE'S BEING FUNNY SHE'S GOT ANOTHER THING COMING...
OKAY, CALM DOWN. I WANNA ASK YOU SOMETHING...

...HAVE YOU CHECKED YOUR ROOM TO SEE IF ANY OF HER STUFF IS MISSING?
HUH? NO, WHY SHOULD I? WHAT'S THE POINT?
JAY, WHO—

JUST DO IT, ALL RIGHT?
=SIGH= ALL RIGHT. HANG ON...

WHAT'S UP?
I'LL TELL YOU LATER...

...I COULDN'T FIND ANYTHING. ALL OF HER CLOTHES ARE GONE...
=SIGH=. WELP, THERE YA GO. THAT OUGHTA ANSWER ALL OF YOUR QUESTIONS.
FLUMP!

?!? WHAT QUESTIONS? WHAT THE FUCK ARE YOU TALKING ABOUT—
SHE'S LEFT YOU, YOU MORON! CAN'T YOU GET THAT THROUGH THAT THICK SKULL OF YOURS?!?

...STAY PUT, I'M COMING OVER. =CLICK!=
ARRRGH...

AND SO...

...GROANNN... GIMME A BREAK...

...I CAN'T BELIEVE IT... I JUST NEVER SAW IT COMING... ≥SOB≤

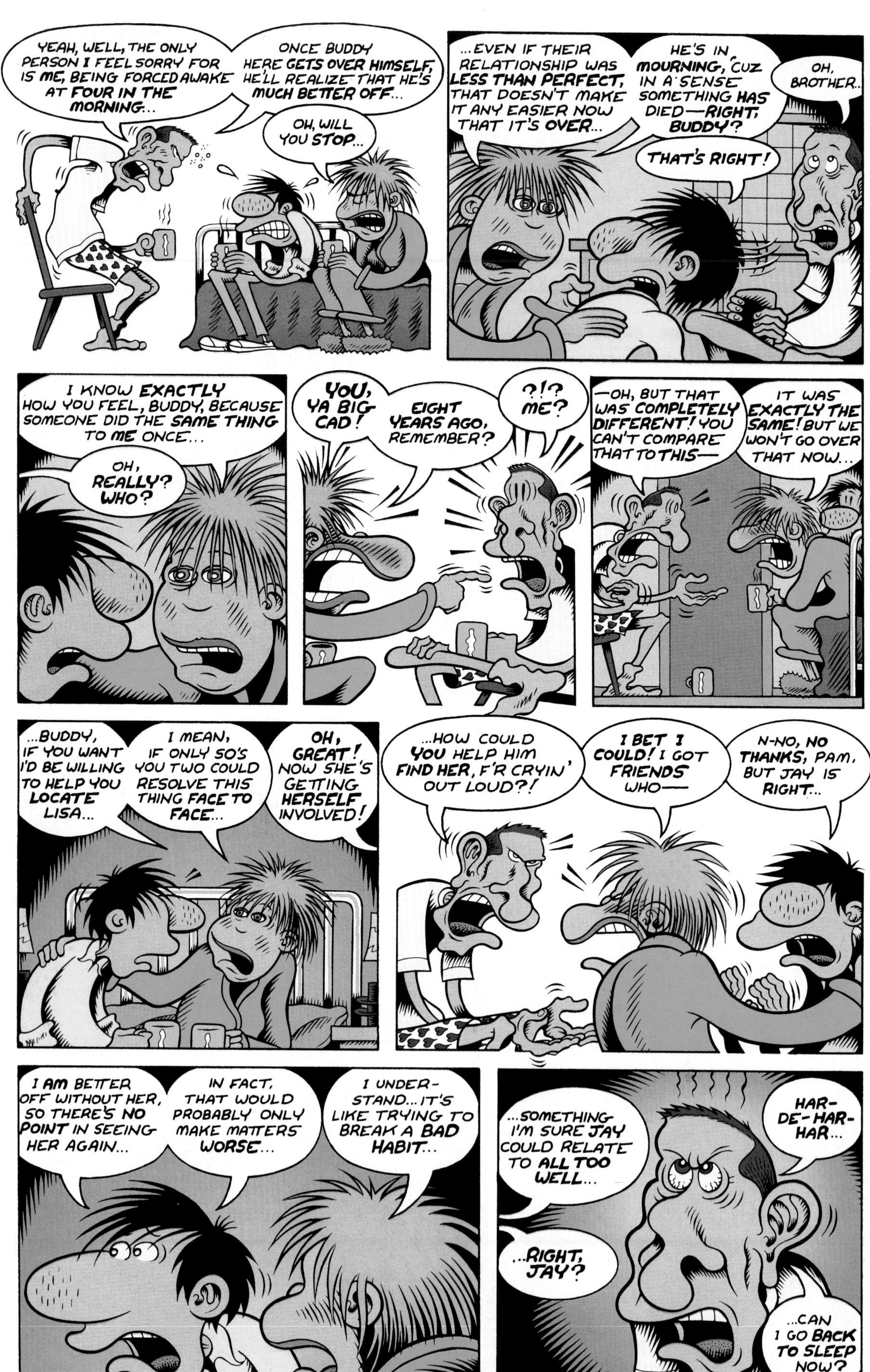
YEAH, WELL, THE ONLY PERSON I FEEL SORRY FOR IS ME, BEING FORCED AWAKE AT FOUR IN THE MORNING...
ONCE BUDDY HERE GETS OVER HIMSELF, HE'LL REALIZE THAT HE'S MUCH BETTER OFF...
OH, WILL YOU STOP...
...EVEN IF THEIR RELATIONSHIP WAS LESS THAN PERFECT, THAT DOESN'T MAKE IT ANY EASIER NOW THAT IT'S OVER...
HE'S IN MOURNING, 'CUZ IN A SENSE SOMETHING HAS DIED—RIGHT, BUDDY?
OH, BROTHER...
THAT'S RIGHT!
I KNOW EXACTLY HOW YOU FEEL, BUDDY, BECAUSE SOMEONE DID THE SAME THING TO ME ONCE...
OH, REALLY? WHO?
YOU, YA BIG CAD!
EIGHT YEARS AGO, REMEMBER?
?!? ME?
—OH, BUT THAT WAS COMPLETELY DIFFERENT! YOU CAN'T COMPARE THAT TO THIS—
IT WAS EXACTLY THE SAME! BUT WE WON'T GO OVER THAT NOW...
...BUDDY, IF YOU WANT I'D BE WILLING TO HELP YOU LOCATE LISA...
I MEAN, IF ONLY SO'S YOU TWO COULD RESOLVE THIS THING FACE TO FACE...
OH, GREAT! NOW SHE'S GETTING HERSELF INVOLVED!
...HOW COULD YOU HELP HIM FIND HER, F'R CRYIN' OUT LOUD?!
I BET I COULD! I GOT FRIENDS WHO—
N-NO, NO THANKS, PAM, BUT JAY IS RIGHT...
I AM BETTER OFF WITHOUT HER, SO THERE'S NO POINT IN SEEING HER AGAIN...
IN FACT, THAT WOULD PROBABLY ONLY MAKE MATTERS WORSE...
I UNDER-STAND... IT'S LIKE TRYING TO BREAK A BAD HABIT...
...SOMETHING I'M SURE JAY COULD RELATE TO ALL TOO WELL...
HAR-DE-HAR-HAR...
...RIGHT, JAY?
...CAN I GO BACK TO SLEEP NOW?

THE NEXT EVENING...
BARGE!
OH MAN, WHAT A DAY...
...STAY TUNED FOR "COPS" —RIGHT HERE ON FOX!

?!?
WHAT TH—
HEY, BRO'! AND CONGRATULATIONS!
CHIPS

"CONGRAT-ULATIONS"? FOR WHAT?
BABS TELLS ME LISA FLEW THE COOP— IS THAT TRUE?

...YEAH, I'M AFRAID SO...
SO, THEN YOU'RE A FREE MAN! CAUSE FOR CELEBRATION IF EVER THERE WAS ONE!

I-YI-YI...
PLUS MOM'S GONE FOR THE ENTIRE WEEK-END, SO THE PLACE IS OURS TO DO WITH AS WE PLEASE...

WHADAYA MEAN, "WE"?
HEY, THIS IS MY HOME JUST AS MUCH AS IT IS YOURS!
JUST BECAUSE YOU LIVE HERE AND I DON'T...
BOLT!

IN FACT, NOW THAT THE POPULATION OF THIS PLACE IS STARTIN' TO THIN OUT, I'M THINKIN' I MAY JUST MOVE MYSELF BACK IN...
OH, SWELL...
—AHOY, MATIES! IS THIS WHERE THE PARTY BE AT?
...BAD BOYS, BAD BOYS... WHACHOO GONNA DO...

—C'MON IN, JIMMY! YOU CAME TO THE RIGHT PLACE!
JIMMY FOLEY?! WHAT ARE YOU DOING HERE?

WHAT AM I DOING HERE? WHY, WORD ON THE STREET IS THIS IS BACHELOR PAD U.S.A.!
OR HAVEN'T YOU HEARD?
NO, I HAVEN'T HEARD!

OH, I GET IT. POOR LI'L BUDDY HERE WAS PLANNING ON SULKING ALL WEEKEND BY HIMSELF, NOW THAT HIS GIRL-FRIEND'S DITCHED HIM!
OH, SO NOW THE WHOLE WORLD KNOWS ABOUT ME 'N' LISA, HUH, BUTCH?
HAW!
RUB! RUB!
DING! DONG!

—OH NO!
WELL, LOOK WHO'S HERE! IT'S "JAKE THE SNAKE" AND HIS SIDE-KICK "PENCILS"!
WHA' UP, BRO?
YO, WHAT BE HAPPENIN'?
ALL RIGHT, PENCILS! YOU BROUGHT SOME "BUGLES"! YOU DA MAN!
BUGLES

...HEY BUDDY, WHERE YA GOIN'?
LIKE JIMMY SAID, I'M OFF TO SULK FOR THE REST OF THE WEEKEND...

(HEY, WHAT'S WITH YOU, MAN? I MEAN, LISA WAS OKAY 'N' SHIT, BUT YOU KNEW IT WASN'T GOIN' NOWHERE!)

(ADMIT IT, MAN, YOU'RE BETTER OFF, AN' YOU KNOW IT!)
OKAY, I'M "BETTER OFF"! NOW IF YOU'LL EXCUSE ME...

SLAM!
...HUH. PATHETIC...
SWIG!

HOURS LATER...

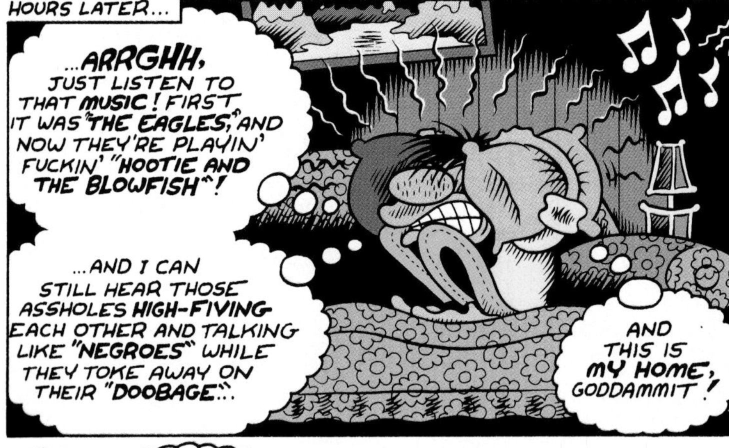
...ARRGHH, JUST LISTEN TO THAT MUSIC! FIRST IT WAS "THE EAGLES," AND NOW THEY'RE PLAYIN' FUCKIN' "HOOTIE AND THE BLOWFISH"!
...AND I CAN STILL HEAR THOSE ASSHOLES HIGH-FIVING EACH OTHER AND TALKING LIKE "NEGROES" WHILE THEY TOKE AWAY ON THEIR "DOOBAGE"...
AND THIS IS MY HOME, GODDAMMIT!

THIS HAS GOT TO BE THE LOWEST POINT IN MY LIFE...
ALL THIS AGGRAVATION, AND FOR WHAT?
I MEAN, JEEZ-IZ!

THIS IS ALL LISA'S FAULT, GODDAMN HER...
FOR THREE YEARS I PUT UP WITH ALL OF HER HANG-UPS AND CRAZINESS...
AND THEN SHE JUST UP AND LEAVES ME TO WALLOW IN MY WRETCHED-NESS AND DESPAIR...

...I SHOULD FIND OUT WHERE SHE IS, TRACK HER DOWN AND STRANGLE THE LAST OUNCE OF LIFE OUT OF HER...
SHAKE!
SHAKE!

...AND THEN I'D ASK HER IF SHE'D COME BACK TO ME...
-SOB!-
-CHOKE!-

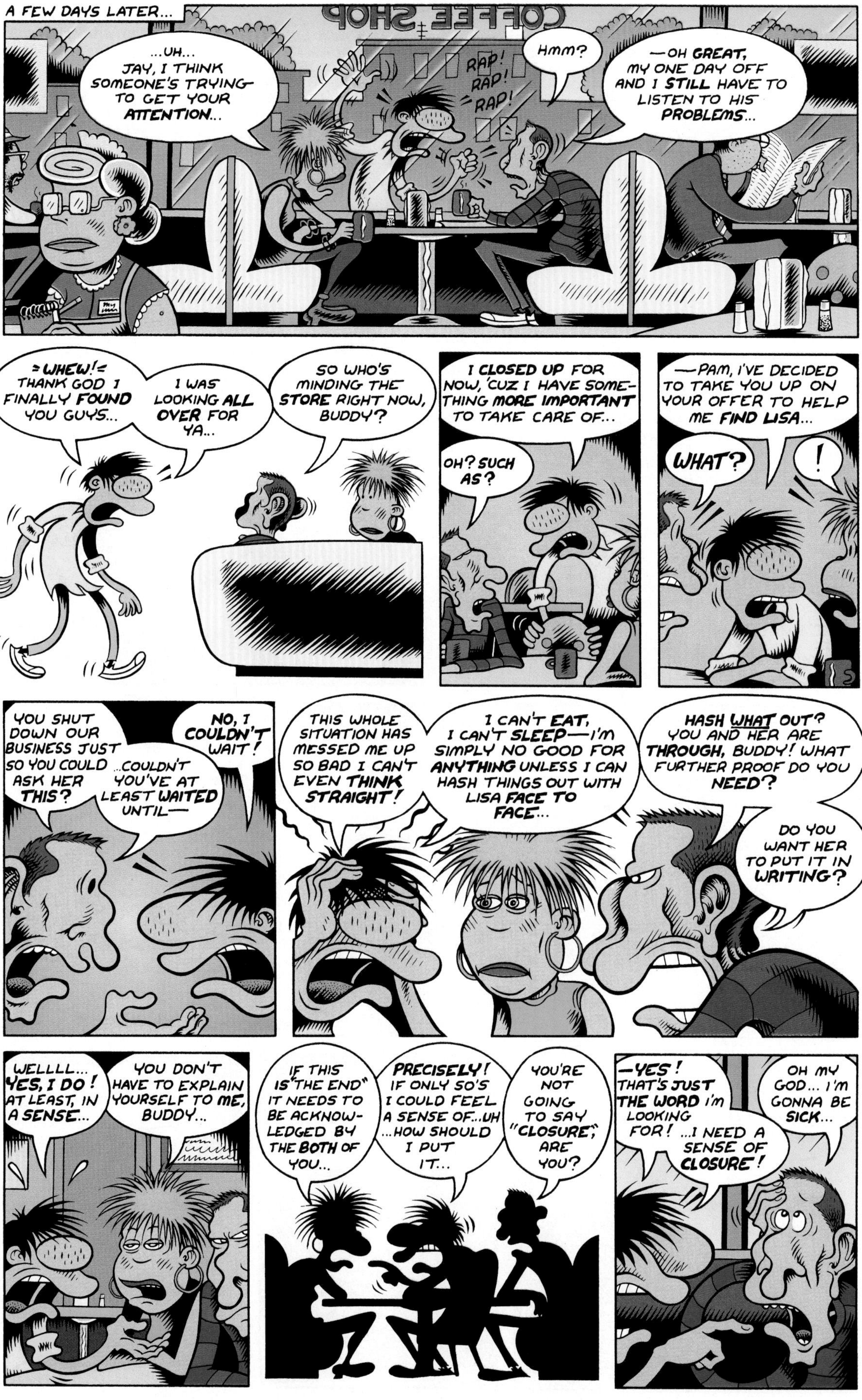

A FEW DAYS LATER...
COFFEE SHOP
...UH... JAY, I THINK SOMEONE'S TRYING TO GET YOUR **ATTENTION**...
RAP! RAP! RAP!
HMM?
—OH **GREAT**, MY ONE DAY OFF AND I **STILL** HAVE TO LISTEN TO HIS **PROBLEMS**...

=**WHEW!**= THANK GOD I FINALLY **FOUND** YOU GUYS...
I WAS LOOKING **ALL OVER** FOR YA...
SO WHO'S MINDING THE **STORE** RIGHT NOW, BUDDY?
I **CLOSED UP** FOR NOW, 'CUZ I HAVE SOMETHING **MORE IMPORTANT** TO TAKE CARE OF...
OH? SUCH AS?
—PAM, I'VE DECIDED TO TAKE YOU UP ON YOUR OFFER TO HELP ME **FIND LISA**...
WHAT?
!

YOU SHUT DOWN OUR BUSINESS JUST SO YOU COULD ASK HER **THIS**?
...COULDN'T YOU'VE AT LEAST **WAITED** UNTIL—
NO, I COULDN'T WAIT!
THIS WHOLE SITUATION HAS MESSED ME UP SO BAD I CAN'T EVEN **THINK STRAIGHT**!
I CAN'T **EAT**, I CAN'T **SLEEP**—I'M SIMPLY NO GOOD FOR **ANYTHING** UNLESS I CAN HASH THINGS OUT WITH LISA **FACE TO FACE**...
HASH **WHAT** OUT? YOU AND HER ARE **THROUGH, BUDDY!** WHAT FURTHER PROOF DO YOU **NEED?**
DO YOU WANT HER TO PUT IT IN **WRITING?**

WELLLL... **YES, I DO!** AT LEAST, IN A **SENSE**...
YOU DON'T HAVE TO EXPLAIN YOURSELF TO **ME**, BUDDY...

IF THIS **IS** "THE END" IT NEEDS TO BE ACKNOWLEDGED BY THE **BOTH** OF YOU...
PRECISELY! IF ONLY SO'S I COULD FEEL A SENSE OF...UH ...HOW SHOULD I PUT IT...
YOU'RE NOT GOING TO SAY "**CLOSURE**," ARE YOU?

—YES! THAT'S **JUST THE WORD** I'M LOOKING FOR! ...I NEED A SENSE OF **CLOSURE!**
OH MY GOD... I'M GONNA BE **SICK**...

OKAY, MS. HARRIET-THE-SPY, NOW THAT YOU'VE BEEN RECRUITED FOR THIS ASSIGNMENT, HOW DO YOU INTEND TO PULL IT OFF?
ERR, YEAH, I'M KINDA CURIOUS ABOUT THAT AS WELL...
THAT'S EASY...
FIRST, ALL WE GOTTA DO IS ASK LISA'S FRIENDS AND ACQUAINTANCES WHERE SHE MIGHT BE, FOR ALL WE KNOW SHE MIGHT HAVE TOLD SOMEONE!
I ALREADY DID ASK, NOBODY KNOWS ANYTHING...
THINK THEY'RE HOLDING OUT ON ME?

MAYBE, MAYBE NOT. BUT SOMEONE'S GOT TO KNOW SOMETHING...
YA JUST GOTTA ASK THE RIGHT QUESTIONS, LIKE WHO SHE WAS LAST SEEN WITH, WHAT KIND OF "SCENE" THEY'RE INTO...
WHAT KIND OF DRUGS DO THEY TAKE...

EXACTLY.
>GASP!< OMIGOD! WHAT IF SHE'S HOOKED UP WITH A BUNCH OF DRUG DEALERS? THIS COULD BE DANGEROUS!

PFFT. I DOUBT IT. THOUGH YOU NEVER KNOW...
GEE PAM, ARE YOU SURE YOU WANNA DO THIS? I REALIZE IT'S A LOT TO ASK OF YA...

ARE YOU KIDDING? THIS IS GONNA BE FUN! I ALWAYS WANTED TO BE A DETECTIVE ANYWAY...
WHO KNOWS, IF I PULL THIS CAPER OFF MAYBE I'LL START MY OWN BUSINESS...
SWELL. JUST DON'T GET ME INVOLVED IN ALL THIS. I DON'T HAVE THE STOMACH FOR IT.

FINE. YOU'D JUST GET IN THE WAY, ANYWAY...
—OH, AND THAT REMINDS ME...

...BUDDY, IF I'M GONNA DO THIS, IT'S GOTTA BE ON MY OWN...
YOU'RE GONNA HAVE TO STAY OUT OF THE PICTURE...
REALLY? BUT...WHY?!

BECAUSE YOU'RE TOO DESPERATE! YOU'LL SCARE PEOPLE OFF!
ME? WHY? WHAT WOULD THEY BE AFRAID OF, THAT I MIGHT KILL HER OR SOMETHING?

WELL... YEAH!
BUT... BUT...

...ARRRGHH!

AND SO...

...WELP, HERE WE ARE, AT "GOTH CENTRAL STATION"...

THIS IS **IT**? IT LOOKS LIKE MY **MOTHER'S HOUSE**!

1437

FIFTEEN MINUTES LATER...
...SIT ON A PICKLE! DO AS I SAY! YOU DRUGGED-UP, BALD-HEADED BASTARD...
YES, RABBI STERN! =CHORTLE!=
CLICK!
ARRGHH... SHUT-UP, HOWARD STERN,...
YOU'RE NOT FUNNY TO ME TODAY...

...THEN AGAIN, NOTHING SEEMS FUNNY TO ME THESE DAYS...
...SHIT, WHAT'S TAKING HER SO LONG? ARE THEY HAVING A TEA PARTY IN THERE OR WHAT?

...I SHOULD JUST BARGE RIGHT IN THERE, GRAB THE FIRST "DEATH ROCKER" I SEE BY THE THROAT, AND SQUEEZE THE INFO I WANT OUT OF HIM...
AFTER ALL, IT'S MY LIFE THAT'S BEEN RUINED! I HAVE THE RIGHT TO BEHAVE INAPPROPRIATELY IF I WANT TO...

...UGH, THIS IS EXCRUCIATING! I DON'T THINK I CAN SIT STILL FOR ANOTHER MINUTE...

...PERHAPS I'LL JUST SNEAK AROUND THE SIDE OF THE HOUSE, AND TAKE A PEEK AT WHAT'S GOING ON INSIDE...

...I KNOW I'M BREAKING MY PROMISE TO PAM, BUT WHAT HARM COULD IT DO?
THEY'RE ALL ENGAGED IN CONVERSATION, ANYWAY, SO NO ONE'S GONNA NOTICE ME...

...HUH. THERE SHE IS, YUCKIN' IT UP WITH SOME STUPID "GOTH" COUPLE...
...WHOSE SIDE ARE YOU ON ANYWAY, PAM?!?

..HMMMM... NO ONE'S IN THE BACKYARD...

...AND WHADAYA KNOW—THE BACK-DOOR'S OPEN! FANCY THAT!

...NO SIGNS OF LIFE SO FAR, EXCEPT FOR SOME MUSIC EMANATIN' FROM THIS BEDROOM DOOR...
RIDERS ON THE STORM...

?!?
HELLO, WHAT'S THIS?!?

BARGE!
AH-HAH! SO THIS IS WHERE YOU'VE BEEN ALL ALONG!
GET UP, YOU NO GOOD—
...ZZZZZZ...
THE
CRO

...WHUH?! WHO THE HELL ARE YOU, MAN?
?!?
—OOPS! SORRY! I, UH...

?!? WHAT'S ALL THAT SHOUTING ABOUT?
HEY JOE! WHAT'S GOING ON BACK THERE?
UH-OH... I HOPE IT'S NOT...

HEY, WHO IS THIS GUY!?
GOOD QUESTION!
THAT'S WHAT I'D LIKE TO KNOW!
OH NO!
I-I CAN EXPLAIN...

TH-THIS IS THE FELLOW I WAS JUST TELLING YOU ABOUT...
?
Y-YOU MEAN, THIS IS LISA'S BRAIN-DAMAGED COUSIN?
L-LOOK, NO OFFENSE, BUT GET HIM OUT OF HERE, OKAY?

C-CERTAINLY... WE'RE ON OUR WAY...
?!
THANKS AGAIN, AND I'M REALLY SORRY ABOUT ALL THIS...
YEAH, SURE. DON'T MENTION IT.
("BRAIN-DAMAGED COUSIN"?)
(SHHH!)

..."BRAIN-DAMAGED," HUH? HE JUST SEEMS LIKE YOUR RUN-OF-THE-MILL PSYCHOPATH TO ME...
DO YOU THINK WE SHOULD WARN LIZZIE ABOUT THEM?
NAH. WHY SHOULD WE?

...BESIDES, SHE STILL OWES US BACK RENT.
FLUMP!
PROPAGANDA

I MEAN, IF SHE STILL HASN'T BOTHERED TO WRITE OR CALL YOU AFTER ALL THIS TIME, I CAN'T SEE WHY YOU WOULD EVEN CARE ANYMORE...

I KNOW, I KNOW...

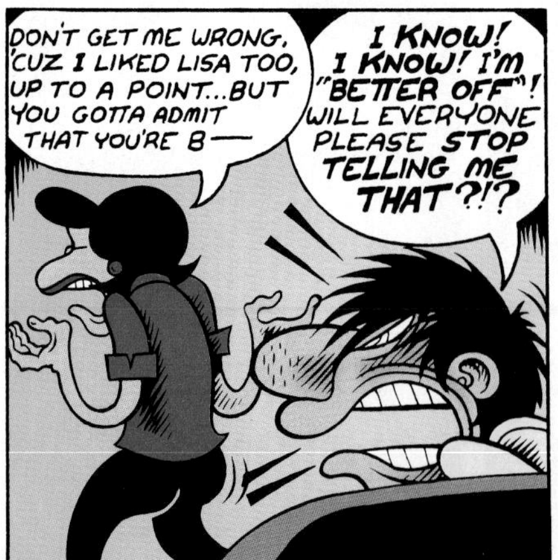

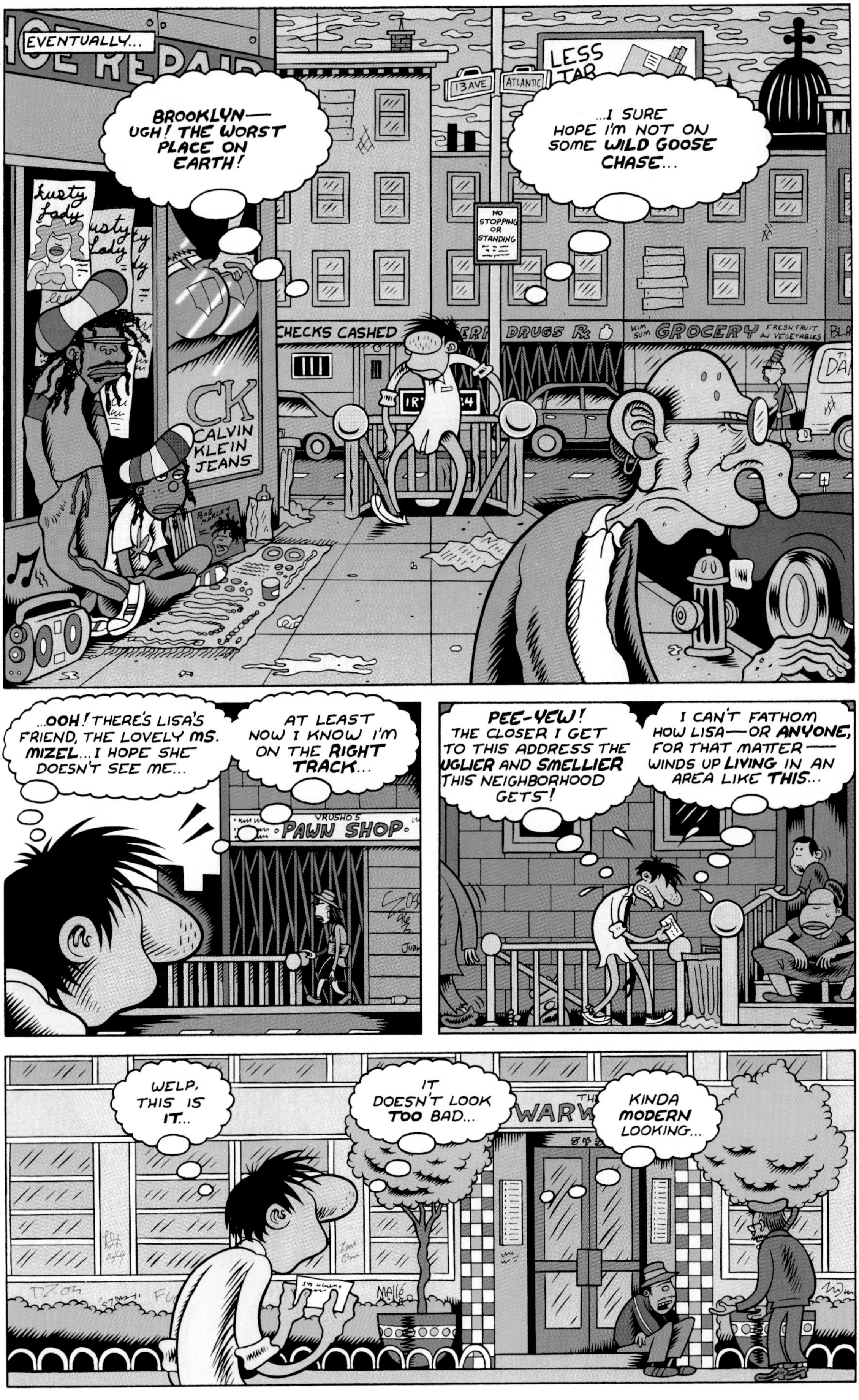

EVENTUALLY...
BROOKLYN— UGH! THE WORST PLACE ON EARTH!
...I SURE HOPE I'M NOT ON SOME WILD GOOSE CHASE...
SHOE REPAIR
13 AVE
ATLANTIC
LESS TAR
NO STOPPING OR STANDING
CK CALVIN KLEIN JEANS
BOB MARLEY
CHECKS CASHED
DRUGS
KIM SUM GROCERY FRESH FRUIT AN VEGETABLES

...OOH! THERE'S LISA'S FRIEND, THE LOVELY MS. MIZEL... I HOPE SHE DOESN'T SEE ME...
AT LEAST NOW I KNOW I'M ON THE RIGHT TRACK...
VRUSHO'S PAWN SHOP

PEE-YEW! THE CLOSER I GET TO THIS ADDRESS THE UGLIER AND SMELLIER THIS NEIGHBORHOOD GETS!
I CAN'T FATHOM HOW LISA—OR ANYONE, FOR THAT MATTER— WINDS UP LIVING IN AN AREA LIKE THIS...

WELP, THIS IS IT...
IT DOESN'T LOOK TOO BAD...
KINDA MODERN LOOKING...
THE WARW

TWO-AND-A-HALF DOZEN DOORS LATER...

L-LISA?! IS THAT YOU?!?
UH-HUH. C'MON IN!
...IT'S OKAY, PABLO. HE'S A FRIEND.
MARILYN MANSON

SO WHA'DYA DO, HIRE A DETECTIVE TO TRACK ME DOWN? =SNICKER!=
ER, N-NO, I... THAT IS, I JUST ASKED AROUND...

PABLO, WILL YOU TURN DOWN THE MUSIC, PLEASE? THANKS.
THAT'S QUITE A NEW LOOK YOU'RE SPORTIN' THERE, LISA...

...YOU EVEN GOT A TATTOO, I SEE...
UH-HUH. YA LIKE IT?
MARILYN MANSON

I, UH...
NEVER MIND... FORGET I EVEN ASKED...

SO, IS THIS YOUR OWN PLACE?
I MEAN, ARE YOU RENTING IT OR JUST "CRASHING"?
SORTA BOTH...

...IT'S LIZ'S MOTHER'S PLACE. PABLO'S HER STEP-BROTHER...
UH-HUH...
MORRISSEY

HER MOM'S A REALLY COOL LADY, AND SHE'S TOTALLY WILLING TO LET US STAY AS LONG AS WE WANT TO...
BUT WE'D STILL LIKE TO GET A PLACE OF OUR OWN, EVENTUALLY...
BY "WE", DO YOU MEAN YOU 'N' LIZ?

HMM? WELL.... YEAH.
I SEE...

WELL, THIS IS A PRETTY NICE PLACE, ALL THINGS CONSIDERED... BUT WHAT'S UP WITH THAT SMELL DOWNSTAIRS?
SMELL? OH, THAT'S PROBABLY LEFT OVER FROM THE DEAD GUY...

?!? "DEAD GUY"?
YEAH, SOME GUY CRAWLED INTO THE LOBBY ONE NIGHT 'N' JUST ...DIED...
HE MUST'VE WET HIM-SELF WHEN HE EX-PIRED...
KNOCK! KNOCK!
I'LL GET IT...

...THE SUPER SAYS HE CAN'T GET THE SMELL OUT OF THE CARPET, THOUGH WE KINDA DOUBT THAT HE EVEN TRIED...
HEY, HOMES. WUSSUP?
NUFFIN'. WUSSUP W'CHOO?
BAP!
HE NEVER FIXES ANYTHING...
SO I NOTICED. THE FRONT DOOR'S BUSTED, TOO...

SO, LIKE, WHAT ARE YOU DOING FOR MONEY THESE DAYS? DO YOU HAVE A JOB ALREADY?
NO, NOT YET. RIGHT NOW MY ONLY SOURCE OF INCOME IS FROM ROLLING THESE JOINTS FOR PABLO AND HIS FRIENDS TO SELL IN THE PARK...

LICK!

I KEEP SCANNING THE WANT ADS, BUT THERE'S NOTHING OUT THERE, UNLESS I WANNA WORK FOR BASKIN-ROBBINS...
THEY'RE ALWAYS HIRING FOR SOME REASON...
YO, LISA, WHACHOO GOT? WE'RE HEADIN' OUT...

THEY'RE IN THAT TRAY OVER THERE, BOYS...
...I'M IN NO RUSH, THOUGH, SINCE THE MONEY I MAKE FROM DOING THIS IS PRETTY DECENT...
(WHA, DOES SHE MEAN THIS TRAY?)

...IS THIS ALL YOU DONE TODAY?
'FRAID SO. SORRY.

(MAN, THAT BITCH BE A SLOW ROLLAH)...
(THAT'S 'CUZ SHE'S DOIN' TOO MUCH YAKKIN', IS WHAT IT IS)...
?

OH WELL, WE'RE OUTTA HERE...
THAT'S RIGHT, GET TO WORK, YOU "BITCHES"...
(SHH! BUDDY, STOP!)

BUT—
(THEY DON'T MEAN ANYTHING BY IT, THEY JUST LIKE TO ACT TOUGH, IS ALL)...
(JUST LEAVE 'EM ALONE)...
(WHO IS THAT OLDSTER, ANYWAY?)
(I'M NOT SURE, BUT I GOT A HUNCH)...

SLAM!

...SO... YOU PROBABLY WANNA KILL ME, HUH?
UMM... KINDA...
...WHAT WAS IT THAT FINALLY MADE YOU SPLIT FOR THE CITY, LISA?
WAS IT SO'S YOU COULD SEE "MARILYN MANSON" AT THE SPUR OF THE MOMENT?
MARILYN MANSON
WELL, YEAH, PARTIALLY...
...I MEAN, LET'S FACE IT, BUDDY, I HAD NO BUSINESS LIVING OUT THERE IN THE SUBURBS WITH YOU 'N' YOUR MOTHER...
I SHOULDA NEVER MOVED OUT THERE WITH YOU IN THE FIRST PLACE...
I TRIED TO WARN YOU...
AND YOU WERE RIGHT! I ADMIT IT!
I'M JUST SORRY I DIDN'T LISTEN!
SIGH
...BUT EVEN STILL, LISA, IT ISN'T ALL THAT BAD OUT THERE IN THE 'BURBS...
OY VEY! YOU'VE GOT TO BE KIDDING!
FLUMP!
...LOOK, BUDDY, BY NOW I'M SURE THAT EVERYBODY'S TOLD YOU THAT YOU'RE BETTER OFF WITHOUT ME, AND THEY'RE RIGHT...
...BUT IF YOU REALLY, REALLY DO WANT ME TO COME BACK I'LL AT LEAST CONSIDER IT, OKAY?
I MEAN, THAT IS WHAT YOU CAME HERE TO ASK ME, RIGHT?
ERRR... YEAH, BUT...
BUT WHAT?
BUT AT THE SAME TIME IT'S BECOME PRETTY OBVIOUS THAT WE'RE A LOST CAUSE, Y'KNOW?
I MEAN, WHAT'S THE POINT, RIGHT?
...YEAH... I SUPPOSE...
MARILYN
—SAY, YA WANNA SMOKE A JOINT WITH ME?
HUH? OH, SURE!
...IS THIS STUFF ANY GOOD?
WHAT, THESE LOLLIPOP STICKS? NAH, IT'S GARBAGE...
HERE, I'LL ROLL A BIG FAT ONE, JUST FOR US...
—WOW! SO I GET TO DO THE "HONORS," HUH?
HEH-HEH...
UH-HUH. THIS IS JUST LIKE SMOKING A "PEACE PIPE" FOR US, ISN'T IT?
TEE-HEE!

EPILOGUE...

KEEP OUT!
STAN FREBERG WITH
JUXTAPOSE sold Here
TONIGHT ONLY
WANTED:

>AHEM!<
HMM? OH, I'M SORRY, CAN I HELP—

...OH... IT'S YOU...
YOU'VE GOT A LOT OF NERVE, YOU KNOW THAT?

I DO? I—
LISA'S BEEN SUPER DEPRESSED EVER SINCE THAT DAY YOU DECIDED TO PAY HER A "VISIT."
...YOU REALLY LAID A GUILT TRIP ON HER, DIDN'T YOU?

I DID? I—
Y'KNOW, IF YOU CARED ABOUT HER AT ALL YOU'D JUST LEAVE HER ALONE AND MIND YOUR OWN BUSINESS!

...WHAT YOU DON'T SEEM TO REALIZE IS THAT THIS IS THE REAL LISA NOW—SOMEONE YOU'VE NEVER REALLY KNOWN, LET ALONE WOULD'VE APPRECIATED...
WINNIE THE POOH

...SO DON'T WASTE YOUR TIME LOOKING FOR YOUR POOR LOST LITTLE GIRLFRIEND ANYMORE, BECAUSE SHE DOESN'T EVEN EXIST! UNDERSTAND?!?
S-SURE! LOUD AND CLEAR!

GOOD! GLAD TO HEAR IT!
GOODBYE, "BUDDY"!

SLAM!

SHRUG!
SHRUG!

THE COMPLETE BUDDY EXPERIENCE...
BUDDY GO HOME!
BUDDY GO HOME! (HATE #16-20): The first color issues! Buddy and Lisa hightail it back to NJ. (128 pp. $16.95)
NEW JERSEY OR BUST
VOL. IV OF THE COMPLETE BUDDY BRADLEY STORIES FROM HATE!
BY PETER BAGGE
BUDDY THE DREAMER
BUDDY THE DREAMER (HATE #6-10): The "grunge-rock" issues... What more need be said? (128 pp. $12.95)
VOL. II OF THE COMPLETE BUDDY BRADLEY STORIES FROM HATE BY PETER BAGGE
ALCOHOL FUNNYCAR DEC. 11th AT THE OFFRAMP
FUN WITH BUDDY + LISA
FUN WITH BUDDY AND LISA (HATE #11-15): The fun-loving couple sinks deeper into degradation. (128 pp. $12.95)
VOL. III OF THE COMPLETE BUDDY BRADLEY STORIES FROM HATE BY PETER BAGGE
HEY, BUDDY!
YO!
WUSSUP?
VALU ARE ALCOHOL FUNNYCAR DEC. 11th AT THE OFFRAMP
VOL. I OF THE COMPLETE BUDDY BRADLEY STORIES FROM HATE BY PETER BAGGE!
HEY, BUDDY! (HATE #1-5): Welcome to Seattle! Much fun with Lisa, Val, Stinky, and George. (128 pp. $12.95)
To order with a cred MasterCard), call 1-800-657-1100; go to the web page (www.fanta send via regular mail to FANTAGRAPHICS BOOKS, 7563 Lake Ci WA 98115. Please include $3.00 postage and handling for the book 00 for each subsequent book. Ask for our big 64-page catalog.